Welcome

The 1960s was a decade of triumph and disaster for the traditional British motorcycle industry.

Some milestone motorcycles emerged, machines like the T120 Bonneville 650 and the 750 Norton Commando. These were bikes that left stains on the souls of their (usually young, mostly male) riders.

Today they are recognised as classic icons. The styling of modern Triumph twins designed at Hinckley, and of the new Interceptor 650s from Indian-owned Royal Enfield, pays homage to the magnetic originals. And the classic bike scene, including that old rockers' haunt the revived Ace Café, is thriving.

Yet from 1962 onward the better organised Japanese competition ate up the two-wheeled market, segment by segment. This had begun with Honda's 50cc Supercub and culminated by 1969 with the four-cylinder Honda CB750, the first true superbike. But it was not oriental competition that did for the home industry. That was down to bad management.

There was unwillingness to use profits from boom years to re-tool with modern production equipment. The engines of the BSA and Triumph three-cylinder 750s, our response to the coming Honda-4, were partly built using antiquated belt-driven machinery. There was the absence of coherent forward planning for truly new models, and the failure to create a reliable lightweight. And finally, ironically, it was misguided attempts to extravagantly modernise the industry which broke it financially.

The decade had seen the shift from UK sales in steep decline, to the rapidly growing North American market. For young America motorcycles meant sports, on tarmac, dirt ovals or out in the desert. With US competition feedback and technical input, the Brit bikes' low weight, great handling, sharp looks and storming acceleration got even better, making them the ones to beat.

Meanwhile, in the UK the Triumphs, BSAs, Nortons and Royal Enfields provided unforgettable thrills for the 1960s leather boys. Their wipe-out rate provoked public outrage and was another nail in the industry's coffin. But if you had ever ridden the thunder and snorted hot oil and exhaust fumes as you took it to the limit and beyond, for all their faults, only a British bike would do.
Enjoy the ride!

Editor

Steve Wilson

Contents

Editor: Steve Wilson
Illustration acknowledgements: Garry Stuart. Dan
Mahony Photos. And with grateful thanks for their
help to: John Mitchell, Ariel Owners Motorcycle Club;
Roy Bellett, AJS/Matchless Owners Club; Steve Foden,
BSA Owners Club; Joe Siefert and Andover Norton; and
Royal Enfield specialists Hitchcocks Motorcycles.

Senior Editor: Carol Randall
Email: carol.randall@keypublishing.com
Design: Mike Carr
Cover design: Dan Jarman
Advertising Sales Manager: Brodie Baxter
Email: brodie.baxter@keypublishing.com
Advertising Production: Rebecca Antoniades
Email: rebecca.antoniades@keypublishing.com
Subscription/Mail Order
Key Publishing Ltd, PO Box 300, Stamford, Lincs, PE9 1NA
Tel: 01780 480404 Fax: 01780 757812
Subscriptions email: subs@keypublishing.com
Mail Order email: orders@keypublishing.com

Publishing
Group CEO: Adrian Cox
Publisher, Books and Bookazines: Jonathan Jackson

Key Publishing Ltd, PO Box 100, Stamford, Lincs, PE9 1XP
Tel: 01780 755131
Website: www.keypublishing.com

Printing
Precision Colour Printing Ltd
Haldane, Halesfield 1, Telford, Shropshire. TF7 4QQ

Distribution
Seymour Distribution Ltd
2 Poultry Avenue, London, EC1A 9PU
Enquiries Line: 02074 294000.

We are unable to guarantee the bonafides of any of
our advertisers. Readers are strongly recommended
to take their own precautions before parting with any
information or item of value, including, but not limited
to money, manuscripts, photographs, or personal
information in response to any advertisements within
this publication.

ABOVE *Trouble! The leather boys were loathed. And this shock horror front page brought the law down on them.*

ABOVE RIGHT *Triumph's Anglo-American character – tank badge based on a Buick grille.*

ABOVE *BSA's last and finest 1950s flowering, the 1963 Rocket Gold Star Clubman 650cc twin.*

The Giants
OF SMALL HEATH

IN THE 1950S BSA RULED THE WORLD. THE BIGGEST MOTORCYCLE MANUFACTURER IN BRITAIN, THE BIRMINGHAM-BASED GROUP HELD ALL THE CARDS. WHAT COULD GO WRONG?

From the 1930s through to the 1960s, BSA (Birmingham Small Arms) dominated two-wheeled transport. The group also owned Ariel, Sunbeam, and since early 1951, the Triumph Engineering Company at Meriden, 12 miles away towards Coventry.

The heart of BSA was the 24-acre site at Small Heath, Birmingham 11. It included a canal and rail link, and a sports fields surrounded by a test track. The works were an antiquated rabbit-warren, with the so-called 'New Buildings' completed in 1916. A new apprentice there could get lost in his lunchtime. Much of the production machinery was still belt-driven.

BSA produced most of its components itself, unlike Triumph who bought in. Small Heath had its own foundry, a huge press shop, and a steel works. By the 1950s the 37 group-owned subsidiaries included Jessops, who developed and supplied austenitic high nickel-chromium G2 alloy for BSA's long-wearing motorcycle exhaust valves.

There were also nearby works at Waverley Road, housing BSA's aftermarket accessory company, Motoplas. And 12 miles away in Redditch was the factory where the engines for BSA Bantam lightweights were built until 1970, by which time half a million had been produced. The well-loved Bantams, everybody's first bike, were assembled at Small Heath by a female workforce which had the advantage for management of their being on half the male workers' wage.

FAMILY AFFAIR
Small Heath was famous for its family atmosphere. Often different generations, men and women, from the same families worked at 'the BSA'. The company fostered the atmosphere, with on-site doctors, and a dentist, subsidized canteens, social clubs and sports teams. Outside work hours the formidable works manager, Al Cave, would mow the

ABOVE *Prime Minister Anthony Eden helps celebrate the 100,000th Bantam at the Earls Court Show.*

ABOVE *A bird's eye view of BSA's 24-acre factory site at Small Heath.*

lawns of workers' widows. In the drawing office there was the fragrant smell of the polish applied by the ladies of the finishing department on the floor below. Vermin, mice and rats, abounded, as well as factory cats.

The family atmosphere, and non-militant unions, offset the fact that wages were up to 25% less than for equivalent work in the car industry at nearby BMC Longbridge, or in Coventry. The consequent high turnover of skilled labour did not help Small Heath's quality control.

BSA was a national institution. In World War Two they had survived Luftwaffe attacks and produced the bulk of rifles and machine guns for British forces, plus 126,000 military motorcycles. The sporting BSA Guns survived post-war. Even in the 1960s BSA machines were woven into the fabric of society. Telegrams were

delivered by GPO lads on (de-tuned) red BSA Bantams, 'the clockwork cockerel'. AA patrols were still mounted on yellow BSA M21-powered sidecar outfits. Many police forces were supplied with fleet orders both at home and abroad. So were companies like Shell, the BBC and the Milk Marketing Board.

This workaday image cut two ways for BSA. After a disastrous TT effort in 1921, they had ended the charisma of works racing involvement, and built instead a reputation for reliability. They did thrive in off-road competition however, trials and scrambles, and in the 1950s the great all-rounder, the 350 and 500 Gold Star, became the acme of sports production singles. But Goldies ceased production after 1963. The 1960s were to be a decade when BSA, unlike Triumph, failed to produce a machine that a man would sell his soul for.

BOARDROOM BATTLES
In 1956 there had been a boardroom shake-up, with group chairman Sir Bernard Docker and his brassy wife Lady Norah Docker ousted. The move was orchestrated by Jack Sangster, a canny Scot who had set up the successful Ariel Motor Cycles and Triumph Engineering Company, before selling them to BSA and securing a place on the Board.

Sangster used the Group's 1955 losses, concealed by the Dockers, to remove the couple by November 1956. He re-structured the group, putting Triumph's successful designer/manager Edward Turner in charge of a new automotive division. The group subsidiary Daimler cars was sold to Jaguar, and the bicycle side to Raleigh.

Superficially, Sangster's reorganisation and the return to profitability, with a best-ever year in 1960 when 'Mr Jack' stepped down, were good news. However, there were two drawbacks. The London-based board was now a holding company

ABOVE *The BSA frontage at night on Armoury Road, Birmingham.*

responsible for finance and policy, overseeing a series of wholly-owned subsidiaries. This created a ready-made tool for successors interested only in financial acquisition, rather than decent, reliable products – the essence of the motorcycle industry.

That explained what happened to BSA in the 1960s. At the same time the board made it impossible for experienced

ABOVE *This is the original artwork for the box that the Airfix plastic model C15 came in. Many said it was the only C15 that never leaked any oil.* Pic: *HORNBY HOBBIES*

LEFT *Female BSA workers built and despatched lightweights like the Bantam and, as here, the ill-fated Beagle.*

Triumph's Edward Turner in the saddle of a BSA A65, which as Automotive Division chief he had helped design.

BELOW *An early C15 Star 250.*

an enlarged version, with an upright cylinder, of Turner's unreliable 200cc Tiger Cub. Turner's hastiness in getting the 250 to market, and a reluctance at BSA to question his work, meant that parts were produced without prototype testing. The first thousand C15s had to be recalled.

However, the C15 and its successors, plus its larger 350cc and 441cc variants, though under-engineered, were successful as the basis of World Championship scramblers. They became the sole profitable BSA machine of the 1960s. Over 12 years 97,000 of the 250s were produced and 42,000 of the bigger versions. Turner's magic appeared intact.

middle management to hope for the highest posts. With the board, "there was a firm non-acceptance," wrote the great designer Bert Hopwood, "of practising engineers at the highest level." Journalist Dave Minton summed it up as "hasty, myopic top management, frustrated, overlooked middle management, and a shop floor resentful of their lack of communication."

Sidecar racing ace Chris Vincent was one of three National and World Champion riders working at BSA in the 1960s. The others were trials wizard Sammy Miller after Ariel were moved into Small Heath in 1963, and World Champion scrambler for 1964 and 1965, Jeff Smith. "The gaffers were the last to recognize me," said Vincent, "the ordinary people at the factory knew what I was doing first, and they'd always help."

TURNER TRIUMPHANT?

The second drawback was Edward Turner. He was the designer of the 1937 Triumph Speed Twin and its successors, which had set the pattern for large capacity motorcycles for the next 30 years. But he was now a man approaching 60, suffering from diabetes, with a contract allowing him to spend six months of every year in America. At Meriden he was accustomed to a discreet support network to help overcome his technical deficiencies and make his inspired concepts reality in metal. He was not an ideal appointment to steer the BSA Group giant. "The motorcycle industry," he believed, "has never been big business in the UK."

Sangster had no forward product plan. For 1958 Turner came up with a light, attractive, apparently new unit construction BSA 250 single. This was timely, because the 250 legal limit for learner riders was to become law in 1961. But the C15 engine was basically

Part of the peak profits for 1960 had come thanks to 1959 being the top year ever for new two-wheel sales in the UK, at 331,000. But only just over half of that figure were motorcycles, the rest being scooters and mopeds, mostly imported. And then the British home motorcycle market fell off a cliff, with sales halving by 1962. Cheaper cars and suddenly stiffer hire purchase rates were blamed. So was motorcycling's tearaway image. By 1963 Small Heath had to cancel a factory visit by African dignitaries, embarrassed by acres of shop floor lying idle.

The result was increasing reliance on export. By the early 1960s 90% of BSA's product was going for export to over 150 countries, rising to 288 over the decade. And 70% of that export total went to what was increasingly the golden goose for the industry, North America.

The industry's and BSA's failure to

ABOVE *BSA global export produced some pretty strange customers.*

ABOVE *Fitting a single carb to an A65T Thunderbolt's 'water-melon' engine.*

BELOW *Early A50/A65s suffered from stodgy styling.*

produce a successful modern lightweight was now addressed. Turner announced a group scooter division based in the Waverley works, and designed BSA Sunbeam and Triumph Tigress 175 and 250 scooters. The majority-produced 250 four-stroke twin cylinder engine was a promising design. But with heavy scooters in 1959, the group was entering a limited market at a late stage, as the 1950s scooter boom began to flatten that year.

Turner's 250 handled very well, but it looked and sounded wrong for the two-stroke scooter market. And it suffered from overheating, with vapour locks causing stalling, and passengers burning their legs on the hot side-panels. Turner had failed to calculate the loss of cooling due to enclosure correctly. The project was a seriously expensive failure, with the scooter division quietly shut down in 1965.

A lesser known Turner intervention was his input to the design of the new BSA twins, though an A65 was displayed in the lobby at Meriden. Like Triumphs, the BSA twins had moved to unit construction from 1962/63. Unit engines were cheaper to build, but the decision to go unit was also in response to demands for tougher machinery from the States, where competition was king.

The unit BSAs' engines featured a tough Triplex primary drive chain and an oversquare engine with tuning potential, but were heavy, and marred by unreliable electrics. Perhaps the short stroke contributed to their severe vibration at speed. Turner was a famous stylist. The A50/A65's lacklustre looks – the Americans called its motor 'the water-melon engine' – seemed like another bid to ensure his Triumph twins remained top dog.

Turner had visited Japan's motorcycle factories in 1960. He had seen their advanced production machinery, providing undreamed-of tolerances, manufacturing consistency, and volume production, and their 1.5 million home market, six times the size of the UK's. He concluded that our industry should concentrate on big bikes, which the Japanese were not yet producing. After a 1962 trade treaty opened the import floodgates, Honda Super Cub step-throughs became an instant success in Britain.

Turner countered with 1963's 75cc BSA Beagle. Its completely inadequate lubrication system caused big

ABOVE *By 1969 with US styling adopted for the range, the A65T Thunderbolt was smarter, but still flawed.*

end failures before 3,000 miles. This provoked mass warranty claims, which BSA refused to honour, leaving their dealers to cover the cost. So, the dealers refused to stock it, and the Beagle was axed in mid-1965. By then Turner had retired as an executive.

THE NEW BREED

Sangster's replacement was the confusingly named Eric Turner, a former aircraft industry accountant with no previous interest in motorcycles. By 1964 the only board member with knowledge of the motorcycle market was Edward Turner's replacement, Harry Sturgeon, another ex-aircraft industry man.

Sturgeon was a skilful salesman who expanded the US market rapidly, with production increasing dramatically at both Small Heath and Meriden. He knew the motorcycle scene, and was the first, in 1964, to alert the group that Honda had their dohc 750-Four, their first really big bike, in the pipeline. He authorized Bert Hopwood and top developer Doug Hele at Triumph, to develop their ohv 750 triple in response, whereas Edward Turner had dismissed it as 'potty'.

Sturgeon also began merging BSA and Triumph sales reps and sometimes dealerships. This diminished brand loyalty, as well as valuable feedback to their factory from reps. It was resisted strongly

in the US where, despite being part of the same group, BSA-Triumph rivalry was understood and relished. Nevertheless, it was a tragedy for the company that Sturgeon fell ill in 1966, dying in April 1967.

The US sales boom meant the group winning the Queen's Award for Industry in 1965 and 1966, and Small Heath production increasing by 40%, with extra manpower hired. From 1965 the factory was also modernized to an extent, with an ICT 1902 computer installed, which controlled a new assembly system, as at BMC Longbridge, via overhead containers. But it was for the assembly of the same motorcycles. As Al Cave confirmed: "In the 1960s, no new tooling of any consequence was put in." Even hydraulic hand tools did not appear until 1967.

The modernisation cost a substantial £750,000 (in today's money, £14.6 million), and began an increased reliance on bank loans, both in the UK and the US. The failure to restrain growth to keep it in line with working capital would be the group's downfall. Meanwhile, in London the board's financiers began a rapid pattern of non-motorcycle acquisitions and disposals. The most unfortunate was the sale of the entire BSA Tools Division to Alfred Herbert and Co. Payment was in Alfred Herbert shares, which when later cashed in cost BSA several million pounds.

ABOVE *BSA Spitfire Mk IV sportster could top 120 – but not for long.*

By 1967 further sales had left motorcycles representing 70% of the group's turnover. The US market continued to be profitable, despite growing Japanese presence there. But its flaw was the complete reliance on a selling season of just six weeks, between April and June. The new breed of executives' attempts to pursue "an academic mission into the primitive backwoods of two-wheel philosophy"

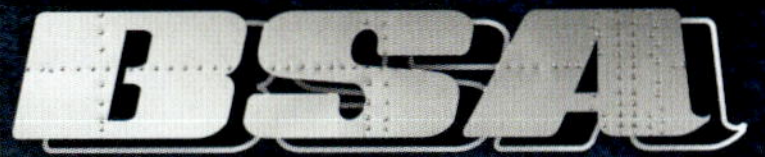

(Hopwood) left them exposed to missing practical necessities like export deadlines. Meetings and paperwork mushroomed, as did expensive consultants. The latter predicted a slump in US demand for 1968. The opposite happened, with BSA severely wrong-footed.

The new breed was exemplified by Sturgeon's 1967 replacement, Lionel Jofeh. Cold, vain and arrogant, he considered Small Heath 'a muck heap'. Not a motorcyclist, his only recorded ride was on 1970's new Ariel-3 50cc three-wheel moped, and he drove that into his own car. He was another man from the contracting aircraft industry, where new models took twice as long to get into production as motorcycles.

TROUBLED TIMES

For 1968 Jofeh authorized a group R and D centre, Umberslade Hall, for all the group's motorcycle design staff, and others. Hopwood and Hele refused to participate. Costing £1.5 million a year to run, it developed a reputation for efforts uncoordinated with production, and the nicknames 'Slumberglades', or 'Mecca', as in, 'they can mecca balls-up of anything there.' The lack of focus and urgency was a significant factor in the disastrous 1971 'New Range'. That was to include only one completely contemporary design, a 350cc dohc twin, the BSA Fury/Triumph Bandit, authorized by Eric Turner to counter Honda's US success, the 305cc CB77 Super Hawk. The 350 would just fail to make it into production.

BSA's watershed year was 1968 when the US selling season was substantially missed. The unit singles, hotted up as the C25/B25 from 1967, and now also badge-engineered as Triumphs, were known for their grenade-like qualities.

ABOVE *BSA went for double page ads for their new three-cylinder flagship superbike for 1969.*

Yet when scrambles champion Jeff Smith reported to one new breed manager that the B25 compared unfavourably to the Suzuki 6, the latter exploded, "We have the Japs beaten for performance, quality and price, and next year we shall butcher them in the marketplace!" The reality was that by the late 1960s, with their proverbial oil-leaks, as they left the factory, all the models BSA offered were under-equipped, poorly made, and unreliable. The new Rocket 3 for 1969, despite impressive performance, was to prove no exception.

BSA group shares had doubled to £2.35 each following the expansion, but with 1969's loss of profits, that year they slumped to 30p. The American BSA and Triumph organizations had been bought out, and a profligate chief executive, Peter Thornton, appointed. Being wholly-owned by BSA, the UK group were now responsible for the very extensive US warranty claims.

Redditch was closing and Waverley Road sold. In Small Heath the situation was chaotic, and the '69 selling season was again mostly lost. The previously quite simple system of incorporating modifications into the flow of production had suffered from computerisation and from Umberslade's haphazard interventions. An example was the switch from BSF thread forms to US-friendly Unified Thread. The changeover was never completed, creating a storeman's nightmare. A shortage of spares due to concentrated bike production opened the gates to inferior 'pattern' parts, further undermining the former reputation for reliability. And spares were the most profitable side of any vehicle industry.

To chase production again, Small Heath's workforce had risen to over 3,000, and in July 1969 Jofeh announced an abrupt 30% redundancy. The cost of tooling up for the triple, Umberslade, expensive modifications to the A65 engine, and the US reorganisation, meant that group profits fell by 75% to just £½ million. Hopwood predicted that "our 1971 model year will be a disaster" and resigned as an executive in January 1970, staying on to assist the racing effort.

As the Swinging Sixties ended, the giant was already tottering. Years later, however, sidecar champion Chris Vincent would say of Small Heath, "It probably wasn't run very well, but us in Birmingham that had to do wi' 'em were soft on the place."

ABOVE *The twins' computer-controlled production line, clearly showing containers holding components.*

AJS and Matchless
IN SOUTHEAST LONDON

AWAY FROM THE ENGINEERING POWERHOUSES OF THE MIDLANDS AND NORTH, THE LONDON-BASED AMC GROUP PLOUGHED THEIR OWN FURROW WITH A PROCESSION OF WELL BUILT MACHINES.

The basis of AMC (Associated Motor Cycles) was Matchless Motor Cycles. Founded in 1902 by the Collier family, they had been winners of the singles' class of the first ever TT races. Matchless were the only volume motorcycle producer based in London rather than the Midlands and the North, with the Plumstead Road factory in industrial Woolwich known locally as 'Colliers'.

In 1931 they had taken over the Stevens' brothers' AJS company (Albert John Stevens), also TT winners, and moved production down from Wolverhampton to Woolwich. After World War Two the two marques were badge-engineered to be virtually identical, though differing in detail and styling. AJS was promoted as the sporting marque for the 1940s and 1950s works road racers.

These were the exotic supercharged AJS Porcupine, and the 350 7R ohc single, smoother and lighter than the 350 Manx Norton. It dominated the junior class of domestic road racing, even after the company withdrew from the sport in 1956 and ceased racer production in 1962. AMC were also successful with both marques in the ISDT, trials and scrambles, with works versions of their ohv 350 and 500 singles. Matchless later became the competition marque, with the 500 version of the 7R badged the Matchless G50. This was because the name was better known in the majority US market.

Matchless had made the money to go racing from their work in World War Two. One of their employees, Jock West, had ridden for BMW in 1939, coming second in the Senior TT to his German teammate Georg Meier, on supercharged 750 twins. These advanced machines featured hydraulically-damped telescopic forks, in the age of girders. It is thought that West, before enlisting as an RAF bomber pilot, had a hand in supplying a set of these forks to Plumstead.

ABOVE *Matchless wartime G3L 350, the basis of AMC's post war fortunes.*

Matchless were already providing the British forces with a good girder-forked WO G3 ohv 350. Plumstead now radically lightened it and added their own adapted version, with lighter alloy sliders, of the BMW fork, which they dubbed the 'Teledraulic'. By 1941 this created the G3L, the first tele-forked army machine, and very much the Forces' favourite. Some 80,000 wartime G3 models were produced. But there had been a price. The youngest Collier brother, Bert, was killed in 1941 riding a production BMW they had got hold of, which he crashed on his way to work.

The G3L was the basis of the 350 and 500 Matchless G3/G80 and AJS Model 16/Model 18 heavyweight singles. These sold well until the mid-1950s, when the market for these reliable but weighty machines flagged – just 302 350s were produced in 1955. The company tried a 'Lightweight' 250 and 350 from 1958, but these were not successful, partly due to the 250's 325lb weight and bulbous styling. The singles had been joined by a 500 twin, designed by Phil Walker, with

a couple of ingenious features, for 1949, and more would follow. Their story will be found in the 'AMC Twins' chapter.

MORE MARQUES

The Associated Motor Cycle name had been adopted in 1937 when Matchless had taken over the prestigious Sunbeam marque, though they soon sold it on to BSA. Postwar in 1947 they bought Coventry-based Francis-Barnett, and in 1951 James in Birmingham, both manufacturers of good quality, Villiers-powered lightweights. Then in 1953 they took over the ultimate famous name in British motorcycling, Norton, who remained in their traditional Bracebridge Street, Birmingham home.

The money for all this had come from war work, including procedures like the War Department post-war selling G3L spares back to the factory by pound weight – while continuing to order new ones. AMC did tell them, but the practice continued. And 1945 profits of £80,000 were invested into the racing machinery, rather than pay tax on it.

LEFT *The short production line of handsome, well-rated 1959 Trials singles at Plumstead.*

BELOW *1958's 100 mph Matchless G11 CSR 600 was more like what young riders wanted.*

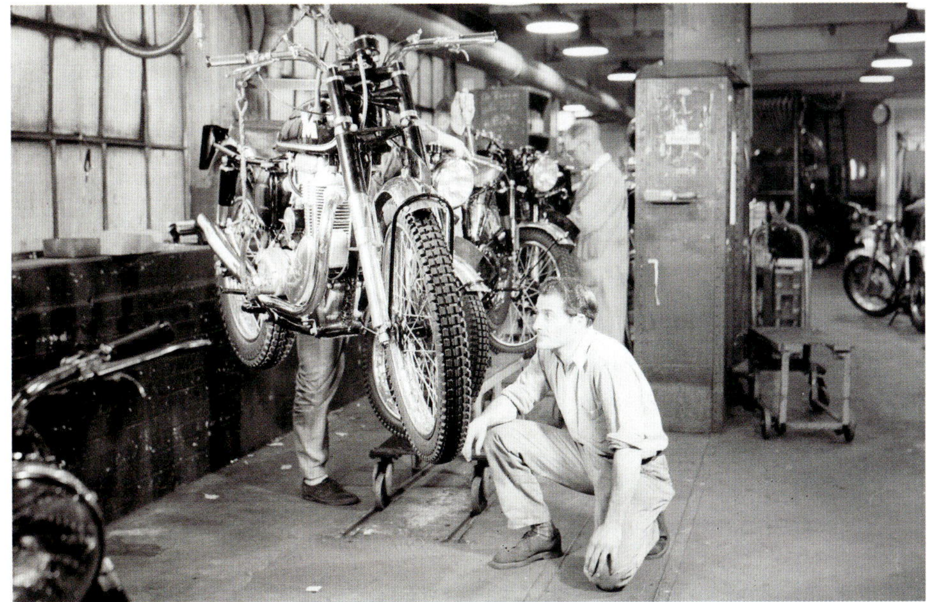

But from day to day, AMC like the rest of the industry existed on tiny profit margins. "Profits were made on spare parts, not machines," wrote draughtsman Vic Webb. All sorts of things were given to the manufacturers – Dunlop tyres at below cost price, oil and petrol tank caps by the oil companies as the caps advised the use of their brand, free spark plugs and chain on the assumption that owners would replace worn items with the same kind. "The Colliers had a vast knowledge of the cost and characteristic of materials, so the cheapest way of manufacturing a component at an acceptable quality could be found." But the last Collier, Charles, died in 1954.

The core management after that consisted of managing director Donald Heather, Jack Kelleher, a butcher by trade who had married a Collier daughter, and Arthur Sugar, the company accountant. Heather was a seasoned motorcyclist who regularly rode the company's products. But, already in his 60s, he was a man who had dismissed scooters as 'a fad', and believed that motorcyclists enjoyed de-coking their cylinder heads over the weekend. Pre-war he had been sacked from *Motor Cycling* magazine. Resentful of the press, for some years he refused to release machines to them for road tests, which was scarcely a sales aid.

Short-sightedly, the interest for these men was solely in profit for the shareholders, who included themselves. "For management, it was all about the money," confirmed road-tester Harry Winch. Under their regime, models substituted agonizingly incremental detail changes for true development. The result, as a correspondent in the AJS/Matchless Owners Club magazine *'Jampot'* pointed out, was that "it's no good trying to fit an 'interim' back

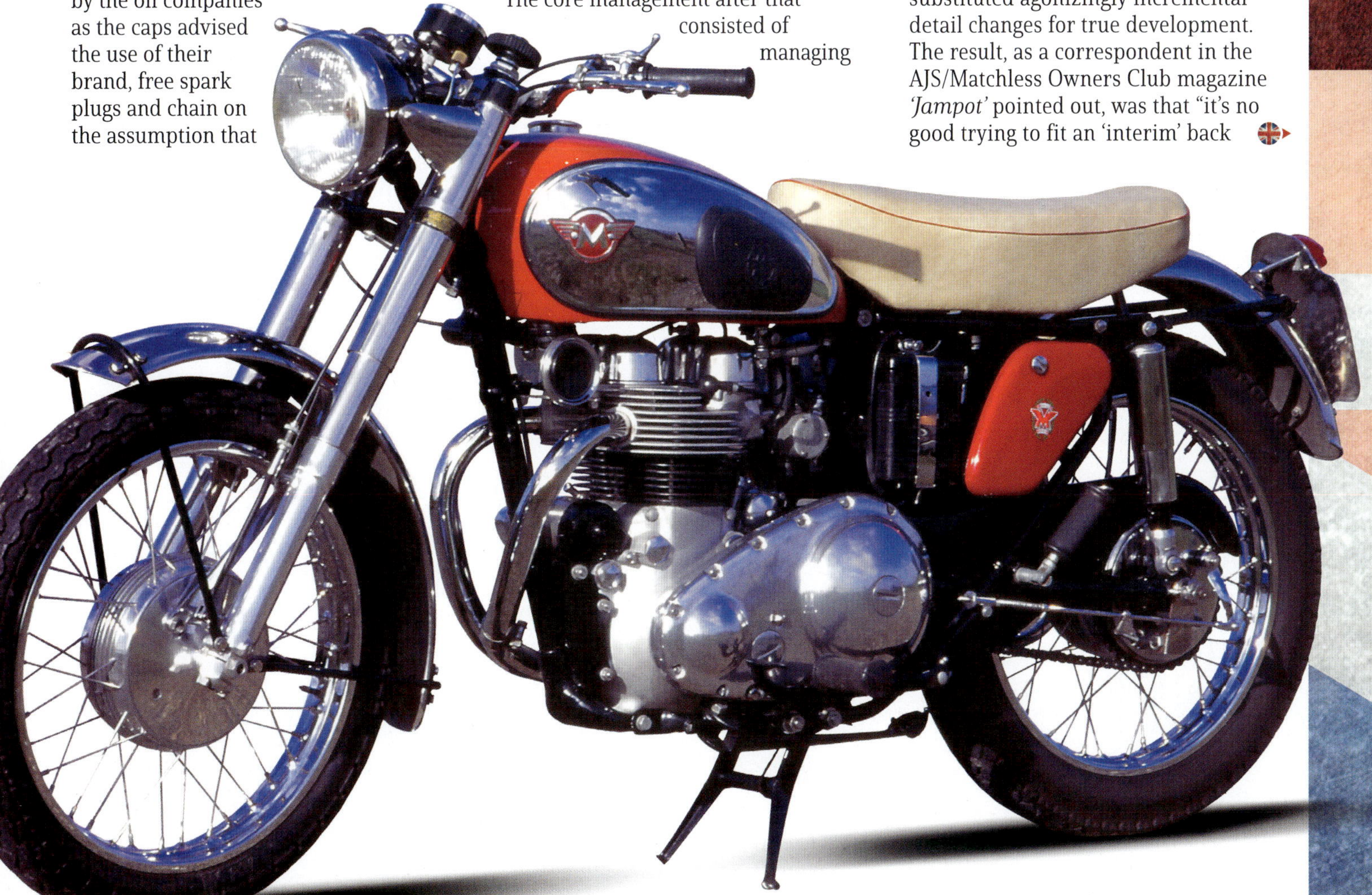

ABOVE *A typical Matchless G80 500 Heavyweight single with AMC's own tubby 'Jampot' suspension units. They appealed to older riders.*

wheel to a pre-'63 frame, or '57 – '62 Girlings (shock absorbers) to any other year frame, or a '55 sub-frame to any other frame at all!"

PLUMSTEAD PRIDE

The factory employed between 1,000 and 1,500 workers and produced an average of 15,000 machines a year. And paradoxically, despite the lack of real development, it was a place of exactingly high standards of finish. There was skill, loyalty, and pride in work.

The highly regarded three-coat stove enamelling was said to have derived from the ownership of Sunbeam, the old industry standard for fine finish. All handlebars were skilfully bent on a hand-operated capstan. The number of quality control personnel, up to 130, exceeded other factories. Very few machines came back for service under warranty.

Yet not until the mid-1950s, on the Teledraulic forks, was the bodge of the BMW-type yokes onto the frame's front diamond improved. And the Teledraulic's

narrowness dictated the use of just a seven inch sls front brake on powerful 650s until the mid-1960s. And the meticulous standard applied to the 500 twin's production was said by PR man Ray Kennard to mean that it had been produced at a loss since Day One.

The factory layout was also not ideal for manufacture. It consisted of three floors and the roof-top. The main production shop was on the ground floor. Frames were prepared on the first floor, along with the paint and cadmium plating

in the mid-1950s. Heather then spent a further £1/2 million, firstly on the design and manufacture of the company's own gearbox for 1957. This was an outstanding product, also used on Nortons, though Jock West stated that it cost more to make than it did to buy in units from their previous supplier Burman.

Secondly, after a foolish falling-out with two-stroke engine manufacturer Villiers, in 1956 AMC commissioned their own range of two-stroke engines from Italian designer Vincent Piatti. They began to build an extension of the factory to house their manufacture, but this was blocked by the Council. The engines proved unreliable, principally because their

LEFT *Plumstead around 1964, Matchless competition singles await rectification before despatch.*

ABOVE *1963-on 'knee-knocker' badges say it loud – AMC's heart was Matchless.*

ABOVE *Matchless Trials singles get full attention despite Plumstead's basic facilities.*

facilities. The tool room and tool services were on the third floor, while frames were assembled in huts on the roof. So machines went in lifts from the top to the first floor, then back up to the second for rectification after road-testing, and finally down again to the ground floor warehouse to await despatch.

Yet despite being dark, grimy, cramped and antiquated, the factory could be a rewarding place to work. Inter-departmental friction was non-existent, or at least limited to the fiercely contested cricket series. "Cricket was the great thing down there," recalled Harry Winch. "Along with the Chrysanthemum Society, parties for the kids at Christmas, and home-grown rock bands like The Ajays on stage in the canteen."

As one ex-welder put it: "The majority of employees had pride in their product. The benefit of this (inter-departmental)

co-operation was that every employee could see the end result of everyone's efforts, and new models were often displayed in the factory canteen… co-operation often ironed out any problems in production." Union action was rare until towards the end, in the mid-1960s. The racing effort was popular, with an annual coach party leaving early on Thursday morning for the Isle of Man Senior TT, though they had to be back again for work on Saturday morning.

As well as the wartime windfall, Plumstead's reputation meant that it continued contract work for Rolls-Royce and Ford at nearby Dagenham. The latter returned the favour when problems arose around 1960 with the twins' nodular iron crankshafts. This income stream, and that of Norton, allowed plant and machinery to be kept up to date, with an estimated £1 million spent

'laminar flow' system required precision machining and assembly, and Plumstead had no experience with two-strokes. In 1961, humiliatingly, AMC had to return to Villiers and get them to assemble the remainder. As Plumstead works convenor E. 'Tiger' Smith put it, Heather had: "spent a lot of money for nothing."

CRASH AND BURN

Another expensive failure in 1959 had been buying the Indian name in the USA from Brockhouse. The Southport, Lancs firm had acquired it when Indian had gone under in the early 1950s. They used it to market Royal Enfield and other British marques, including AMC. Heather now bought the name and used it in an attempt to market AJS/Matchless in the burgeoning US market. Norton under Bert Hopwood were left to make their own arrangements. They did this

ABOVE *The uninspired styling of a standard late 1950s G12 Matchless 650.*

LEFT *A 1965 AJS Model 33 CSR 750, with Norton Atlas engine in an AMC chassis, it features Norton Roadholder front forks and an eight inch front brake.*

successfully via the Joe Berliner Corps, while AMC's Indian Sales Corporation lost £80,000 in its first year. Berliner soon became the AMC distributor in the now-majority US market, and largely dictated what Plumstead produced.

Meanwhile, in 1960 there had also been a failed attempt to relocate AJS/Matchless to a new facility on the Isle of Sheppey, Kent. More money was lost paying an architect to design the new factory.

Then in 1960 the coming home market slump threatened what was by then the firm with the longest unbroken record of motorcycle production in the industry. With profits shrinking, Heather, now 70, announced his retirement as managing director in August 1960, but stayed on as chairman. Symbolically, the legendary three-coat paint finish was reduced to two. Then, when a loss of £350,000 came for 1961, shareholders at an Extraordinary General Meeting in June tried to sack all the board bar Jock West. They narrowly failed, with Kelleher and

Sugar remaining as joint MDs. Jock West resigned later in the year.

In 1963 AMC mortgaged the James and Francis-Barnett factories, having moved the latter in with the former the year before. In Trojan Horse style, they set up Suzuki (GB) to sell the Japanese marque in Britain, to the disapproval of the rest of the industry. And early in 1963, after Hopwood had resigned and gone to Triumph, the shock news came that Norton and its production equipment had been moved from Birmingham to Plumstead. Only five Norton personnel accompanied the equipment, and there were problems.

Norton man Bob Collier (no relation) got a call from Plumstead to say that the multi-spindle drill which processed Dominator twin crankcases was playing up. Three hundred sets of crankcases had had to be scrapped because the drill for their central bosses wouldn't run true. Collier located the previous Birmingham operator. "Didn't they take the plank with it?" the man asked. The play in the spindle previously had been taken up by wedging a plank against it to stop chattering.

AMC had attempted a 750 version of their own twin, but their design's separate barrels had inadequate metal for this. So, from 1964, the existing Norton 750 Atlas engine was slotted into AMC cycle

parts with Norton front ends. This tended to satisfy no one. Giving all the models names for 1963 was misjudged too, as no one bothered using them.

The factory still contained very talented designers like Jack Williams, and from 1962, Charles Udall from Velocette, plus developers like Wally Wyatt, former Competition Shop chief. The 'comp shop' had often helped improve production models. When the AMC gearbox was introduced, works Matchless scramblers had wrecked several, but with their feedback, better materials had been sourced and it became the best. Wally Wyatt was now working on the 750 Atlas engine and extracting more and more power. That would become the basis of the Norton Commando.

The financial trend continued downwards, however. Some felt that a major cause was hard-nosed Joe Berliner forcing the factory to sell their machines to him for less than the cost of manufacture. Four years of losses culminated in AMC owing their bank £1.25 million. On August 2, 1966 a receiver was appointed, and on September 2 Plumstead, with AMC's marques and manufacturing rights, were acquired by Dennis Poore of Manganese Bronze Holdings. He had already bought Villiers. Delaying the AMC takeover until a receiver had been appointed ensured that there was no benefit for the long-suffering AMC share-holders.

The story of Plumstead from then on will be found in the 'Hybrids' and 'Norton Commando' chapters.

A Decade
OF SUCCESS

TRIUMPH WAS AND PROBABLY REMAINS THE BEST-KNOWN MARQUE OF BRITISH MOTORCYCLE.

In 1935 Edward Turner had been put in charge of the re-branded Triumph Engineering Company, based in Coventry, by Jack Sangster. In 1937 he launched the game-changing 5T Speed Twin 500. His instantly successful engine design was to be the basis of Triumph twins right through until 1988.

Triumph twins were fast, light, flexible enough for town riding, versatile, and as Bert Hopwood wrote: "There wasn't anything delicate about (them)." The engine design featured two pushrods,

ABOVE *Edward Turner relishing America, with Rita Hayworth on his pillion.*

fore and aft, allowing a wide range of valve timing for tuning. Its hemispherical cylinder heads helped produce good acceleration and a lively feel that few of its later rival ohv twins could reproduce, and which riders loved.

Turner, once a motorcycle dealer in South London, had an intuitive feel for what riders were going to want. The Speed Twin was followed by the even more desirable Tiger 100. From then on, demand always exceeded supply for Triumph twins.

MADE IN MERIDEN

As early as 1939 Turner was establishing the marque in America, which he relished. Later his contract would specify

BELOW *Meriden, and a unit T120 Bonneville from 1969.*

that he spend six months of every year there. The Coventry works were bombed out in the blitz of November 1940, but by 1942 the company had moved to a new, purpose-built factory at Meriden, four miles west of Coventry. This new facility gave them a head-start over their competitors' elderly works. Triumph had produced over 40,000 wartime singles,

but with peace, Turner successfully shifted all Meriden's production to twins.

The next major turn he took the product through was the late 1949 move, partly in response to US demand, to 650cc, with the iron-engined 6T Thunderbird. Some Triumph aficionados considered the 650 T'bird to be the optimum Triumph, and that everything which followed was just a misguided attempt to make it go faster!

As Triumph PR man Ivor Davies said: "With Turner the name of the game was money, and at Meriden we made a hell of a lot of it." When Sangster sold Triumph to BSA in 1951 to avoid death duties, the deal included £1/4 million going to Turner directly as 'E.T. Developments,' for his patented designs. Though now part of the same group, rivalry between Triumph and BSA became progressively more bitter from then on.

Turner aimed to build machines that were quiet (by the standards of the day), notably smooth compared to singles, stylish, and good for 20,000 miles without major problems. The latter ambition sounds modest, but it wasn't then, and would take his motorcycles out of the warranty period.

With money saving in mind, E.T., as he was known, would not support works racing. In the TT paddock one day he looked over AMC's exotic works 500 Porcupine twin, and turning to AMC boss Donald Heather, said: "If that's what it takes to win the TT, I'm glad we're dropping out!" The market for production racing was catered for by Triumph's aftermarket speed kits, which carried no warranty liability. Yet the increasingly significant American market was competition-oriented, and this set up tensions, culminating in the ultimate sports roadster, the 1959-on T120 Bonneville. In the 1960s production would swing radically to the US/sporting side.

In the 1950s Turner ran a tight ship, keeping Meriden manning levels down, and limiting annual production to around 25,000 machines. This rose to 30,000 from 1953 when his lightweight Terrier and Tiger Cub models arrived. He had long favoured an 'everyman'-type two-wheeler. He was working along those lines with his enclosed 'Bath-tub' models, starting in 1957 with the 350 'Twenty-One'. With them he hoped to tap into the appeal of scooters with their enclosed mechanicals, and counter motorcycling's growing tearaway image. This and the 500 5TA adopted unit construction engines, with coil ignition. The cost benefits of the latter meant he had already adopted it for the 'cooking' 500s and 650s. The Americans however disliked panelling, and so did younger British riders. The 'Bath-tubs' shrank to 'Bikinis' before being phased out.

THE DOWNSIDE

Turner's pursuit of profitable production came at a price. Triumph telescopic forks, with inside springs, were flimsy. After swinging-arm frames were adopted for 1954, watching Triumph production racers at Brands Hatch, a contemporary reported that "the back of their frames whipped perceptibly – you could see the wheel going out of line." 'Triumphs Don't Handle' and their 'Instant Whip' became proverbial. But the handling was predictable, if you learned never to back off the speed on a bend. And it didn't stop young leather-jackets buying Triumphs because of their speed, style and relative cheapness. Turner let this situation persist.

As an engineer he "seemed to lack the technical knowledge which must be embraced if engine design is to be anything but guesswork," wrote Bert Hopwood, his former and future colleague. Hopwood had painstakingly gained his technical credentials at night school. Turner's inspirations needed a safety net of Meriden subordinates to develop them into workable realities – and to conceal that fact from their egotistical boss.

BSA's development man Dennis Hardwicke was sent from Meriden a set of clutch drawings to work from,

LEFT *A 1961 pre-unit T120 Bonneville – Ride it like you stole it!*

RIGHT *The unit engine T120 Bonneville for 1967.*

and a specimen clutch. The drawings did not relate correctly to the actual clutch. When he queried this, he was told apologetically that he had been sent E.T.'s drawings, not the 'proper' ones. Even the styling details attributed to Turner, the headlamp nacelle and the front number plate shape, had often been refined to their final elegant form by the man he called 'my pencil', Jack Wickes. Wickes wryly referred to his bosses' manner as "amiably bastardial".

Meriden was Turner's comfort zone, and in his 50s he referred to "our little factory in England," when he was making motorcycles in increasing volume for worldwide distribution. His 1956-on

ABOVE LEFT *Edward Turner, as Group Automotive Division chief, bids farewell to BSA stalwart Bert Perrigo.*

ABOVE *The distinctive Triumph headlamp nacelle as fitted to the 350 3TA.*

BELOW *Turner's ingenious 1961 Tina 100cc automatic scooter. It sold quite well after Hopwood had sorted its belt drive.*

spell as BSA Group automotive division chief saw him out of his depth. In 1961 he wrote to Bert Hopwood, asking him to come to Meriden as his deputy.

The two men had clashed when colleagues before. But Hopwood's situation at AMC's Norton, and Turner's assurance that his ill health would mean him stepping down soon, persuaded him. Turner could still be Turner, early on leaving Hopwood to sort out a major technical problem on E.T.'s ingenious 100cc Tina automatic scooter just before its launch, while he departed for America. But with Hopwood soon joined from Norton by his cohort the brilliant 31 year old developer Doug Hele, the three men worked well together on the ultimate pre-unit to unit conversion, on the Triumph 650 engine for 1963. Turner stood down as head of Triumph in 1964, though he was retained as a consultant.

TRIUMPH UNDER THREAT

There then began a refinement of the Triumph 650 and later, 500 twins. Hele addressed the handling issues for 1963, and the front fork the following year. In light of his successful US Daytona racing effort from 1966, he transformed

the engine of the 500. (Until 1969 that was the capacity in America to which overhead-valve racers were still confined by the American Motorcyclist Association (AMA), in support of the larger, home-grown side-valve Harleys.) Benefits from race development, including the best production twin leading shoe front brake, and two-way damped front forks, passed to the road bikes, both Triumph and BSA.

The hub for all this was Hele's Triumph Experimental Department, a tight team of mechanics and developers like Norman Hyde, Les Williams, Henry Vale, Arthur Jakeman and Harry Woolridge. Hele's belief that "there are no gaffers in a technical discussion" was justified by the results gained by his chief development rider and racer, Meriden's irrepressible Percy Tait, on and off the track. Hele "was single-minded," said Harry Woolridge, "he never got stumped. I never saw him side-tracked, even at

ABOVE LEFT *Doug Hele, brilliant Triumph developer and race chief.*

race meetings." This would continue with the triple's racing efforts.

The factory background to this successful period was less happy. With Turner stepping down, there was a growing feeling of being at the mercy of the parent BSA Group. The 1963 closure of the Ariel works at Selly Oak illustrated the ultimate threat (though it was Turner who had done that). Temporary Triumph worker Michael Rea recalled of 1965: "there was a feeling that Meriden's days were numbered, that they were threatened by BSA."

Officials of the factory's eight trade unions identified the BSA Group to the workforce as absentee, un-caring capitalist overlords. Small Heath was judged technically inferior, and the failure of the BSA A50 race teams at Daytona while Triumphs won, reinforced this. Far from appreciating Meriden's achievements, they felt, BSA were actually jealous of them. Later this would seem to be confirmed by a speech at the 1970 Meriden works Christmas party. BSA managing director Lionel Jofeh told the workforce that anyone seen to be favouring Triumph race machinery over BSA would get his cards. Merry Christmas, Mr Jofeh.

Group management

was seen to be lacking in competency and enthusiasm for the specialist area of motorcycles, which their new breed executives referred to as 'consumer durables'. Perceived as simply profit-hungry, they seemed loath to invest in new plant for Meriden. For 1970, £100,000 was spent there on new production machinery, but this was a fraction of the expenditure on Small Heath.

These fears and perceptions were often justified. But the unions' response to them concentrated on extracting the highest possible wage settlements from the bosses. They succeeded, with earnings up to half as much again as the equivalent Small Heath workers.

Resentment at BSA was also fostered when, with sales on the wane, in 1965 production of the lightweight Tiger Cub was moved to Small Heath to become the Bantam Cub. Despite being an improved machine mechanically, this affront to marque loyalty had withered away by 1969. Meriden workers held a mock funeral service for it.

Again, the grenade-like B25 Starfire was also re-badged as the Triumph TR25W for 1968-on, with all variants produced at Small Heath. There were credible tales of BSA line workers spending their lunch hour flicking ball bearings, pebbles and biro caps, at the open spark plug holes of the Triumph versions. They knew that Meriden's reputation, and warranty claims, would suffer. In America unimpressed Triumph dealers called the TR25W "the Twud".

PART OF THE UNION

Meriden was a mile and a half away from the Standard car plant on the outskirts of Coventry. The city had a tradition of trade union militancy. Standard's high wage rates influenced those of Meriden, which became known locally as 'the Bank of England' or 'The Mint'. Agitators dismissed from Standard found work at Meriden. With the 1960s production push, the Triumph workforce rose to around 1,800.

By the late 1960s, union

ABOVE *Triumph's unit Twenty-One 350, with 'Bath-tub' fairing.*

ABOVE *A 1969 single carb 500cc T100S. It became a fine machine after Hele had transformed it via the race effort.*

ABOVE *Triumph 650 'Saint' (Stop Anything In No Time). Police Triumphs helped keep the marque prominent.*

membership at Meriden was compulsory, and there was empire-building between the various unions. Demarcation disputes, about which union's members did what, slowed down the factory's operation. They could lead to stoppages and even strikes. The latter however were unpopular, due to the 1960s' rising standard of living. As one worker explained, "everyone was so committed with HP and mortgages that seven days was a bloody long strike."

Wage demands were something else and spiralled out of control under 1964's new BSA Group managing director Harry Sturgeon. BSA and Triumph management structures were unified that year, Hopwood being passed over with a title of convenience, 'deputy director of Triumph'. Sturgeon had a firm grasp on the necessity of exploiting world markets, especially America, with volume production. Meriden's output rose from 6,300 in 1963 with its depressed home market, to 46,500 in 1967, with 28,000 going to America. Triumph like BSA won the Queen's Award for Export in 1965 and 1966. Later Triumph production reached 900 machines a week.

The unions were not slow to realize that with so much riding on meeting the ten week US selling season, the threat of stoppages could be used to advantage to enforce wage demands. And production-obsessed Sturgeon did not help. On one occasion he burst into pay negotiations between union officials and Meriden's works manager, and impatient at a delay, over-rode the factory management to agree to a rate higher than the one the unions had been demanding! Lionel Jofeh would continue this tendency.

WIN ON SUNDAY

The increase in production came at a cost. Spares manufacture was neglected due to the emphasis on complete machines, and the spares situation deteriorated. Component suppliers like Lucas were hard pushed to keep pace, and incomplete machines stockpiled. When missing components did arrive, the finishing gang were not as expert as the track workers, and reliability could suffer. Storage space for the hundreds of machines became a problem, and motorcycles stockpiled in a marquee on the Meriden lawn suffered

weather damage. But 1967's £7.5 million sales returns were hard to quarrel with.

Triumph men in the 1960s had plenty to be proud of. From 1964, Bonnevilles prepared by the dealer Syd Lawton dominated the production racing scene, winning the prestigious Thruxton 500. Young riders increasingly related to these contests, where the machines resembled the ones they rode, rather than being GP exotica. The racing Thruxton Bonnevilles of the mid-1960s were much admired.

There were also the Daytona victories in 1966 and 1967, and Percy Tait's heroic second place to Agostini's MV at the 1969 Belgian Grand Prix, averaging 116 mph on a special Triumph 500. The culmination was Malcolm Uphill's 1969 victory in the Production TT, with a memorable race average of 99.99 mph. Dunlop re-named their K81 tyre the TT100 as a tribute. But that was a swansong for the 30 year old twin design. From then on the majority of race efforts would go into the triples.

Hopwood and Hele had designed the 750 ohv three-cylinder engine and had a prototype running by late 1965. It was known as 'a Tiger and a half,' as the

ABOVE *A Tiger Cub from 1965, the year it was sent to Small Heath to die.*

ABOVE *The Meriden service department, a centre of skill.*

RIGHT *A T150 Trident 750 triple, with slab-sided looks and 'ray-gun' silencers courtesy of Ogle Design.*

demanding ever-increasing performance for competition, with engine characteristics not always suitable for roadsters. Service Manager John Nelson recorded 'unauthorized clandestine rectification,' when UK customers returned 650s with 'unsolvable vibration'. Their engines would be quietly rebuilt with softer 8.0:1 compression ratio pistons and less lumpy inlet camshafts. It was a fine line to tread between performance, and rideable reliability.

Then there was the 1969 partial introduction of the changeover from BS to UNF thread forms for nuts and bolts. And manufacture of some gearbox

dimensions of its three cylinders had been the same 63 x 80mm as the original Speed Twin. Sturgeon encouraged them but insisted on an ill-judged premature exposure of the barely tested prototype. With his illness, and with US opposition to it as a Meriden rather than a BSA project, it went on the back burner. During this nine month delay, Hele adapted the top end of another of his experimental projects, an improved 500 twin with better breathing. Its squarer 67 x 70

ABOVE *A 1966 6T Thunderbird, once pre-unit cutting edge, and still a fine practical 650.*

LEFT *A 1970 Bonneville, just before the New Range, one of the last and best unit T120s.*

ABOVE *The legendary Mike Hailwood production racing on a mid-1960s Bonneville, the one to beat.*

cylinder dimensions would be adopted for the production triple.

The triple story will be found in Chapter 17. However, some at Meriden would never accept the triple as 'a real Triumph'. The engines of both the BSA and Triumph versions were built (skilfully but laboriously) at Small Heath. The involvement of stylists Ogle, famous for the Reliant Robin, and of Umberslade Hall, did not endear it either. And indeed, despite race wins and record-breaking, it was only when the 1971/72 'beauty kit' restored the T150's looks to 'a proper Triumph', that US sales increased.

TOWARDS END TIMES

"Lionel Jofeh," said Hele, "literally hated Triumph's successes, and seemed quite determined to make Triumph the underdog." From 1968 the buyout

of all four American BSA/Triumph organizations was complete. Sturgeon's failed attempt to amalgamate the US dealers had led to many defecting to the burgeoning Japanese, who now had 2,000 outlets Stateside against BSA/Triumph's 1,600. They were spearheaded by the fast, sophisticated Honda-Four 750 superbike, offered at a cheaper price and in greater numbers than the triple.

Not only were US warranty claims now billed to the UK Group, but the new dealer agreements were of a 'buy on sale or return' kind. In 1968, with the missed selling season, machines, mainly BSAs, were brought back to Britain and sold at a loss of £729,000 (but reduced to £403,151 by the devaluation of the dollar). By 1970, warranty claims were costing Meriden £40,000 a month.

Some of the problems were from the production push increasing manpower to over 2,300, many of the newcomers being unskilled. And some came from the US tail wagging the British dog, in

components to BSA and Triumph twins and the triples, had their production shifted to Small Heath. All this was at a time when production 'was getting crazy' and led to intense frustration at Meriden. The efforts of Umberslade Hall, with Hele and Hopwood having refused to participate, added to Meriden workers' feeling of loss of control over the products they were proud of, and of their destinies.

With the 1971 'New Range' decided upon, while the parent group foundered, Triumph's future was fraught with uncertainty. Yet despite all, with Hele's improvements, the 650s made from 1968 to 1970 are now generally acknowledged to be the apogee of Triumph twins and of 1960s' bikes. They were machines which came alive on bends, with rock-steady handling unimaginable on previous Triumphs. Overshadowed by the triples and the coming New Range, these were the ones where the 1960s sustained development work paid off. They were reasonably priced motorcycles that combined a practical tractability for everyday use with the speed and tautness of race breeding.

Redditch
TO INDIA

OUTSIDE OF THE BSA-TRIUMPH AND AMC GROUPS, ROYAL ENFIELD WERE THE ONLY MAJOR SURVIVOR OF THE BRITISH MOTORCYCLE INDUSTRY. THEY CONTINUED TO PLOUGH AN INDEPENDENT FURROW.

By the 1960s Royal Enfield were the only major independent survivor of the British motorcycle industry. Since 1956 Douglas had been reduced to assembling Vespa scooters. Panther in Yorkshire struggled on, but with the major sidecar market for their sloper singles evaporating after 1960, it closed in 1967. All the smaller two-stroke makers were progressively gutted by Japanese step-throughs after 1962. And if the far eastern competition hadn't been bad enough, their ambitions were knocked on the head completely following 1965 when Dennis Poore took over Villiers and cut off their supply of engines.

Velocette, with a workforce of never more than 150, continued to develop their sporting singles for a small following of enthusiasts. They also produced the 'Everyman' 200cc side-valve LE, though mainly for the police.

Wholly admirable, they could never be major players.

Enfield had been making motorcycles at their Redditch factory 12 miles south of Birmingham since 1902. With a reputation for precision engineering, post-war they carried out work for, among others, the Atomic Energy Commission. They were a family firm, with Major Frank Walker-Smith both chairman and MD. Their head of development, Tony Wilson-Jones, had joined in 1925, an engineer with a keen interest in theoretical matters ('ask him the time and he'll tell you how a watch works'), but he was a rider too.

SINGLE MINDED

Royal Enfield had a reputation as a pioneering company technically. They introduced their cush-hub, adopted by others including Norton, for 1912. Their 'floating' big end design came in

1935. An attention-catching feature was their patented neutral-finder lever, on the marque's Albion gearboxes. And since 1903 they had introduced their trademark dry sump lubrication system, with uniquely, the oil carried not in a separate tank, but in a compartment down in the crankcase. Despite, or because of, Wilson-Jones' technical interests, Enfield machines' tendency to leak oil was never cured. They became known as 'Royal Oilfields'.

Post-war the innovative tendency continued with the 1948-on Bullet 350 G2, a revived pre-war model but now with two-way damped telescopic forks and a swinging-arm frame. Enfield was the first manufacture to adopt what would become, after another six years, the industry's standard set-up. A further sensation came when it was used in competition on the trials and scrambler Bullets. This was a complete innovation,

BELOW *A smart 1960 Constellation.*

ABOVE LEFT *A 1961 Constellation with rare factory racing extras.* INSET LEFT *Determined racer Bob McIntyre had no luck with Enfield big twins.*

ABOVE *Indian-built 350 Bullet, in situ.*

LEFT *Enfield's unique bottom end, with filler cap for the crankcase oil compartment. To its left, patented neutral finder lever on the Albion gearbox.*

which other competitors on rigid-framed machines scoffed at violently, as they thought it would lose grip.

Their top trials rider, 18-year-old Johnny Brittain, arrived in 1950 but got off to a slow start. However, at the tough and prestigious ISDT (International Six Days Trial), rear-sprung Enfields took the manufacturer's award three times between 1948 and 1953. And by 1952 young Brittain had won both the British Experts and the Scottish Six Day trials, and from then until 1957 never looked back.

The Bullet's adoption of a new all-welded frame for 1956, freed up the jigs of the old frame, which were sold to India. From then on the Bullet was manufactured there, at first under licence and then by wholly-owned companies. Like a colonist from Earth on another planet, the 18 bhp single thrived far into the future. Despite material and manufacturing defects, the Bullet's durable nature suited conditions on the sub-continent.

Once the firm had become part of the Eicher Group in the 21st century, quality improved, and a redesigned unit engine was introduced for 2009. In the UK, just 9,000 Bullets had been produced over 13 years. In India, the old Madras/Chennai factory had eventually averaged around 20,000 annually. In 2012, Eicher opened a pair of vast new dedicated facilities outside the city. By 2019 one of them was annually producing over half a million Bullets.

STILL SINGLE

In the UK the Bullet had been followed, as the day of the big single passed, by concentration on a range of 250 singles. They did not succeed in competition, but provided lighter, more responsive bikes for young riders, particularly after the 250cc learner limit had been introduced in 1961. And by 1965, riders aged between 16 and 20 made up 40% of UK motorcycle owners.

The best of these quarter-litres were the 1959-on Sports version of the Crusader. Its gearbox was built in unit with the

over-square (70 x 64.5mm) engine. With a tough one-piece crankshaft, it remained the fastest of the British sporting 250 singles with a top speed of 79mph and a bit more if conditions were right.

In intense cadet rocker street races with BSA's C15 SS80, the Ariel two-strokes and AMC's Lightweight 250s, the Enfield offered stand-scraping handling, though the back end could get skittish on bumpy bends, and the short wheelbase was not to all tastes. The seven-inch front brake was good, a dry weight of 305lb was 45lb lighter than the Bullet, and if they still leaked oil, the deep chrome of the mudguards and of the 3 ¾ gallon tank hit the spot with the leather jacketed L-plate brigade.

With the ultimate Enfield 250, 1965's Continental GT, this youth appeal ceased to be guesswork. Commendably, the firm had turned over the 1963-on Continental, a sports version of the Crusader with a troublesome five-speed gearbox, to selected dealers and to their own apprentices. With the feedback provided, the result was the GT, launched with a 24-hour relay ride by journalists from John O'Groats to Land's End. The ride was interspersed with race-track laps by the likes of Geoff Duke, where the top speed of the GT's tuned 21 bhp engine proved to be around 82mph. The GT's fire-engine red fibreglass tank, dummy cooling rings on the front wheel, clip-on handlebars with grey grips, twinned instruments and fly screen, made it the business for the café racer crowd.

BIG TWINS

Meanwhile, Major Smith had died in 1962, and the large (unrelated) E and HP Smith Group took over. By 1964 they were planning to dismember the old enterprise. With sales of just 6,600 singles between 1963 and mid-'66 as an excuse, in June 1966 Redditch began closing, and the site was sold to the local development corporation. Later Norton-Villiers took a part share in the remaining Enfield Precision company, who were still manufacturing motorcycles.

This strand of production continued in the form of their big twins. The first of these had been the 1953-on 700 Meteor, leap-frogging others' 650s. The 700 twin had been formed by fitting two 350 Bullet top ends side by side, with the barrels separate. This soft sidecar tug had been followed by the 1955 Super Meteor, probably the best of the old bunch.

For the next step in 1959, the heart of the Rocker era, came the Constellation,

essentially a tuned Super Meteor. Dealer Syd Lawton the production race maestro had been impressed with the 118mph he had extracted from a carefully built Super Meteor with a cylinder head adapted to take Gold Star-type valves. The relatively high compression 692cc Constellation featured a similar head.

Unfortunately, the new engine vibrated very badly at speed, despite the strengthened crankshaft being dynamically balanced. It also ran hot, and the inadequate engine breathing system caused oil leaks, as did thin joint surfaces. A further fundamental flaw with Enfield twins was that the engine and its bolted-up gearbox were stressed members of the frame. In combination with the separate cylinders, this eventually led to the crankcases shuffling out of shape.

At the 1957 Thruxton 500 endurance races, Lawton's hard-riding Bob McIntyre had been leading on the tuned Super Meteor, when a split petrol tank reduced him to third place. In 1958 another split tank, together

with a misfire, put him in second place. This had been a bad blow to the marque's street cred among savvy Rockers and didn't reflect well on the Constellation which journalist Dave Minton retrospectively wrote was launched in 1959 "to understandable derision."

This was not helped when Bob Mac, again after leading for some hours, dropped his Enfield twin at that years' Thruxton. The problem this time was Wilson-Jones' new and ineffective 'scissors' clutch. In 1960, despite a redesign, the clutch fouled again and had McIntyre off. Lawton switched to Nortons.

On the street, the 700's strong torque and mid-range acceleration meant that when in tune, exiting a roundabout it could see off even the Bonneville. Its spectacular 4 ½ gallon polychromatic Burgundy and chrome tank, its siamesed exhaust system (which Lawton had found actually slowed acceleration), the adoption of twin carbs for 1960, and a true top speed on production bikes of 110 to 112mph, all appealed. But its reputation as unreliable when ridden hard meant that the Constellation was discontinued in 1963.

BIGGER TWINS

It gave way to the new Interceptor, with an engine bored out to 71 x 93mm giving 736cc. The limited metal which remained for the cylinder walls meant their

LEFT *Daily Mirror front page 'Suicide Club' rider on 1959 Constellation.*

For 1968 the Interceptor Mk IA, in Road Sports and Road Scrambler form, reappeared for the UK. Both now featured coil rather than magneto ignition and were export-styled with a 2¼ gallon tank. They were light for a 750, at 414lb. Around 1,000 were built before the final development, the Interceptor Mk II, arrived for 1969.

The engine had been completely redesigned by Enfield's Reg Thomas, and now featured car-type wet sump

LEFT *Girl Up, on a 1965 Continental GT.*

ABOVE *A Series 1 Interceptor from 1963, photographed outside the Redditch factory.*

LEFT *The US-styled 1969 Series II, with finned wet sump bottom end.*

barrel-to-head gaskets were replaced by Cross metal sealing rings, with partial success in stemming oil leaks.

That was also finally helped by more secure mountings of the engine and gearbox into the open frame, partly via strengthened rear engine plates. In addition, at the rear of the bolted-up gearbox there was now a large alloy block, attaching to the frame and acting as a bracket retaining the box. A revised internal oil system also helped, as did an enlarged sump. Gearing was raised, and the flexible, torquey 52.5 bhp engine could run from 25mph to a claimed 115mph in top gear.

When the Redditch factory closed down, twin production continued in a site 90 feet underground at Upper Westwood, Bradford upon Avon,

Wiltshire. This had been a place where art treasures had been stored during WW2, and secret war work undertaken, which continued with Enfield contract work for the MoD into the 1970s. Testers riding machines up the 500 feet of slanting ramps had to go easy on the throttle so as not to deafen workers in these echoing caves.

The Interceptor's clutch was redesigned, and for 1965 with the US market in mind, the swinging arm was lengthened by three inches to give a rangier 57-inch wheelbase, with fast sweeping bends becoming a pleasure. By now the frames were being manufactured by Velocette. For 1966 and 1967, all Interceptor production was exported. The export styling was impressive, but they still leaked oil when ridden hard, were not fully reliable, and were let down by the ageing Albion gearbox. But the big, powerful, good-handling machines were fun to ride.

lubrication. This was finally to deal with the long-standing problem with the reciprocating oil pump. The latter either over-oiled the bottom end, or at high speeds, cavitated, causing oil to bubble and interrupting its supply to the big ends. Now with a true, finned wet sump, the lubricant was no longer stored in the separate crankcase oil compartment.

With slightly lower gearing and, thanks to the Norton-Villiers connection, Roadholder front forks, carrying either an eight inch SLS or Commando TLS front brake, these last Interceptors suffered few problems. An 800cc version was under development when production, after some 1,800 Interceptors had been produced, ceased in June 1970. A remaining 600 or so Interceptor engines found their way into US entrepreneur Floyd Clymer's Indian-badged, Tartarini-framed twins, and 137 into Rickman chassis, creating an unsatisfactory hybrid.

The Interceptor itself had certainly brought an interesting, individual and powerful variant to the Sixties scene. And the new 2019 Indian-made Interceptor 650, built in their second modern factory, has been a major success.

Modernization and Economy
AT A PRICE

EVERY FIELD IN EVERY ERA HAS AT LEAST ONE MAJOR TECHNOLOGICAL ADVANCE. FOR THE MOTORCYCLE WORLD OF THE EARLY 1960S, THAT MEANT 'UNIT'.

ABOVE A 1963 T120 Bonneville, first year of unit construction. Note clever Triumph design continuity in leaving the gearbox outline visible.

RIGHT A 1966 BSA A65 Spitfire Mk 2, it could be a ferocious vibrator at speed.

The major technical design change on most of the big twins of the 1960s was a move away from engines with a separate gearbox and usually, ignition by magneto and a dynamo for lights. The technical advance was to engines with the gearbox built 'in unit' within their crankcases. Hence machines with separate gearboxes became known retrospectively as 'pre-unit'. The new engines also invariably featured an alternator, mounted on the drive-side end of the crankshaft, to provide power for both the ignition coils, and the lighting and auxiliary electrics.

At first, as with the pre-unit T120 Bonneville, the top of the range machines combined a magneto for ignition with an alternator for the rest. But from 1963 for BSA and Triumph twins the change to alternators was complete.

BRIGHT SPARKS

AMC, including Norton, due to their growing financial problems, never produced 650cc unit twin engines, though prototype versions have subsequently become known. Royal Enfield twins with their low production volumes also stayed with magnetos until 1967. The last big Panther Model 120 slopers had to be produced in 1966 and 1967 with refurbished magnetos, as supplies from Lucas had dried up.

Lucas' most profitable market was in car components. For some years they had wanted to discontinue the complicated manufacture of magnetos for motorcycles, in favour of the simpler and more profitable components of coil ignition systems. Derrick W. Norton wrote that "having been involved with the original design of this" (Lucas 1958 emergency start position on the motorcycle coil ignition system) "...I knew it was intended as an inducement to manufacturers to change from magneto to coil ignition, and little else."

The prime advantage of magnetos was that they were self-contained ignition-spark generating instruments, which provided ignition not dependent on the battery being sufficiently charged. The fact that magnetos were fitted

LEFT A typical pre-unit twin, with its separate gearbox, the Triumph 6T Thunderbird featured an early conversion to alternator electrics in 1954.

in aircraft and marine engines, where failure could be a matter of life and death, spoke volumes. Riders of racing motorcycles also favoured them for their reliability.

The magneto's weak points were mainly limited to their condensers eventually failing, usually due to the 'dielectric' insulating material drying out with age. This meant a major rebuild. More mundanely, they could cause difficult starting if left in the cold, with overnight condensation causing shorting and ignition failure. Gentle application of a hairdryer cured the problem, and once started they were very unlikely to short out in use.

THE LONG HAUL

Edward Turner favoured alternators and coil ignition primarily for the cost-saving. When the system was new, kickstarting the engine could often be easier. But while the system might have been the way forward in car applications, on motorcycles there were several problem areas. The alternator's advantage over the previous 60-watt DC dynamo, which had often used the same drive and was mounted piggy-back with the magneto to form a Magdyno, was its lack of wearing parts. By spinning the magnet on the rotor rather than the coils and having neither dynamo brushes nor a commutator to wear out, the alternator appeared to offer greater longevity.

But almost all British twin motorcycle alternator rotors were fixed to the left end of the crankshaft, and their stator, a ring of coils, mounted in the primary chaincase. As the primary drive chains in there wore, slivers of hardened steel could be picked up by the magnetic rotor and wear the stator. And once the engine began to wear, play in the crankshaft's main bearings could eliminate the necessary five to ten thou. clearance between the stator and the rotor, taking the system progressively out of action.

Another inherent problem of mounting the electrical heart within the engine room, was heat. Ken Craven's 8,000 mile trip around Mexico in 1968 on a BSA A65 outfit, was punctuated by piston seizures, points trouble and lumpy running. He afterwards observed that "the egg-shaped engine mass is a highly efficient heat storage unit – a point against unit construction."

The other main problem was that the early 80-watt, six volt system had no effective voltage control. This was one of the features that would lead Joe Lucas to be known as 'The Prince of Darkness'. The regulator/rectifiers were ineffective, and the system relied on 'switch control' i.e. using the lights and ignition switches to turn off and on the number of coils in the alternator stator which were felt necessary to maintain a fully charged battery. That was an approximate business at best, often leading to the battery overcharging.

A US Triumph dealer recalled that "the 1960 electrics were beyond bad. The Lucas AC generator system lacked proper voltage regulation; a fast ride would cause the battery to boil over. Some batteries were so severely damaged the plates would warp!" And with the coil ignition system, unlike a magneto, that would mean the end of the ride. At the 1961 US Triumph dealer convention, the Lucas rep was introduced as "the man who's trying to put us out of business." It had been meant as a joke, but the unfortunate man was roundly booed anyway.

A more complicated wiring harness was often allied to frequent connection

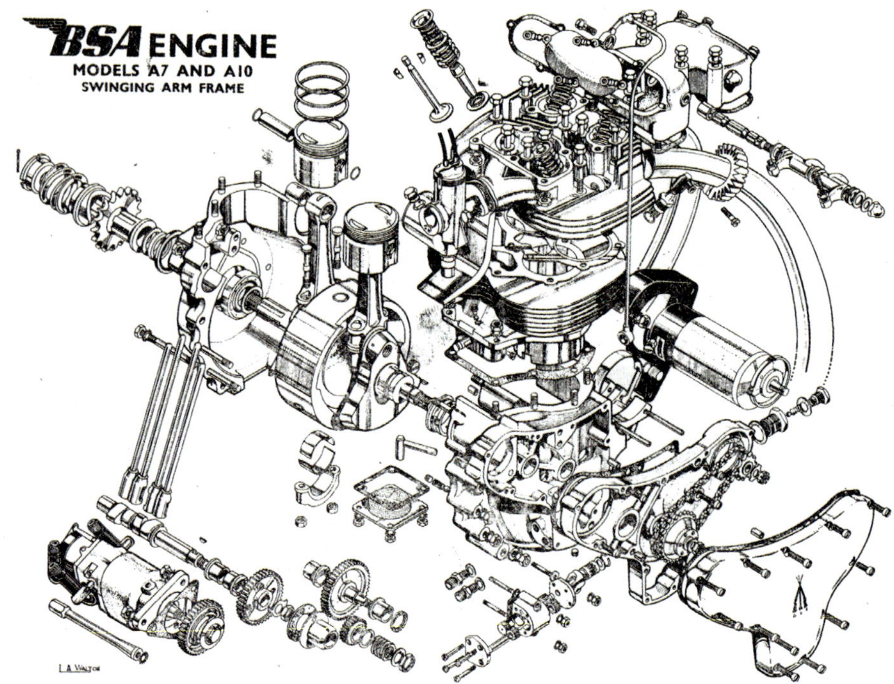

ABOVE AND BELOW *Pre-unit BSA A10 650 engine, and gearbox.*

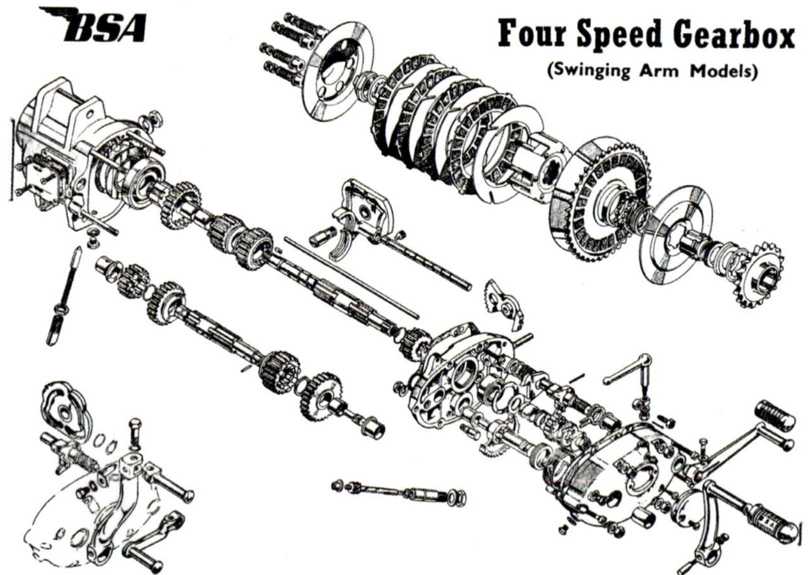

failures. The 4CA contact-breaker points required strobe-light timing to set them up precisely the same for each cylinder. If this was neglected it would mean rough running and increased vibration. These ongoing problems were gradually improved. The electrical systems progressively became 12 volt from 1966, allowing a higher output and improved voltage control via a Zener diode. Then 6CA points with remotely mounted twin condensers, introduced for 1968, allowed independent setting of the contact-breakers for each cylinder. And for 1969, the new Lucas RM21 alternator not only usefully increased output, but also featured resin-encapsulated windings for the stator. This made it significantly less vulnerable both to metal fragments and to heat.

NO FORGIVENESS

A further downside to the crankshaft-mounted alternator was a potential effect on handling. Production race guru Syd Lawton felt that alternator-equipped machines cornering on the limit suffered from the unevenly distributed weight with the alternator stuck on one end of the shaft. Others blamed this for increased vibration. But the general rider was not too concerned.

What did strike many at the time of the changeover to unit construction, was the harsher quality of the new engines. Neale Shilton, a long-time, high-mileage Triumph factory salesman and creator of the unit SAINT 650cc for the police, wrote of his first ride on a new 1963 unit engine: "Within five miles after leaving the factory, I was regretting the change. Vibration had arrived and smooth power transmission was gone."

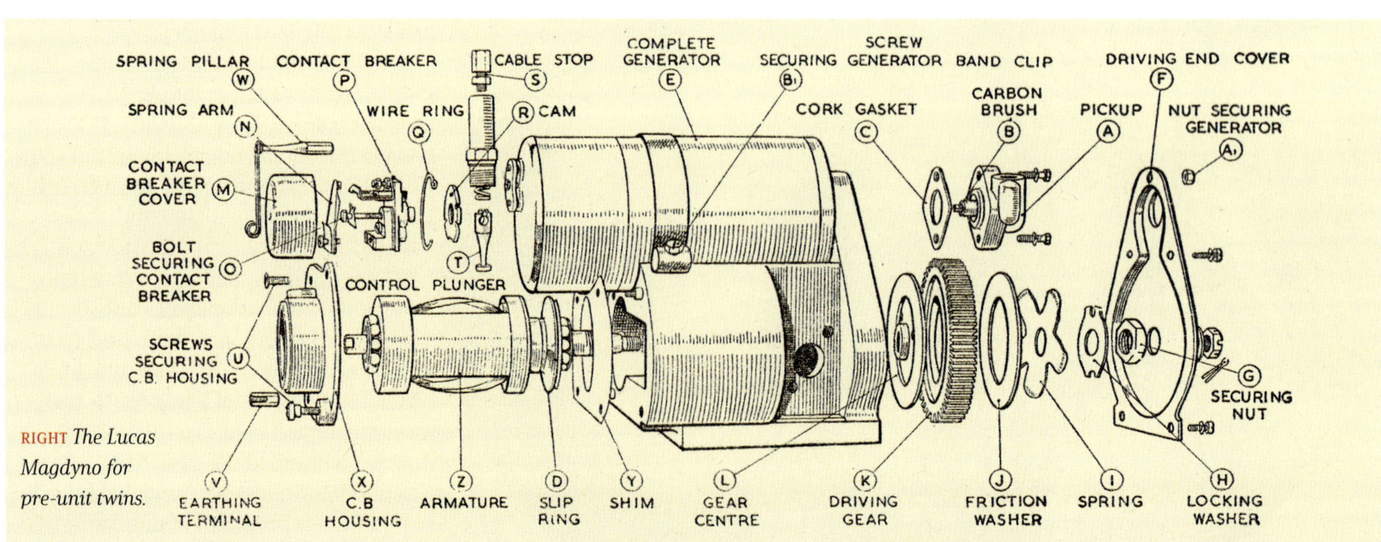

RIGHT *The Lucas Magdyno for pre-unit twins.*

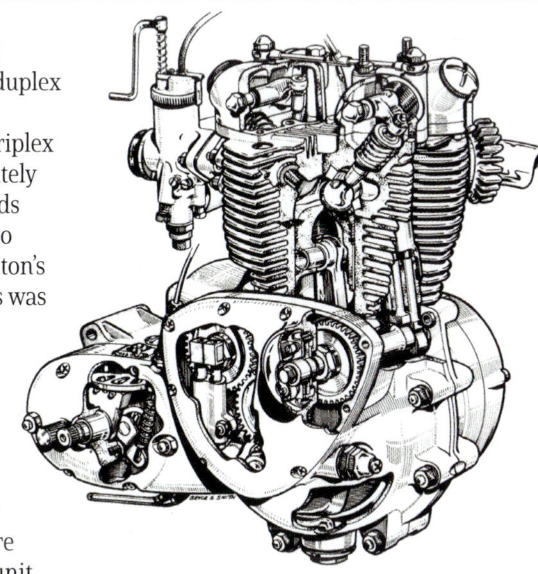

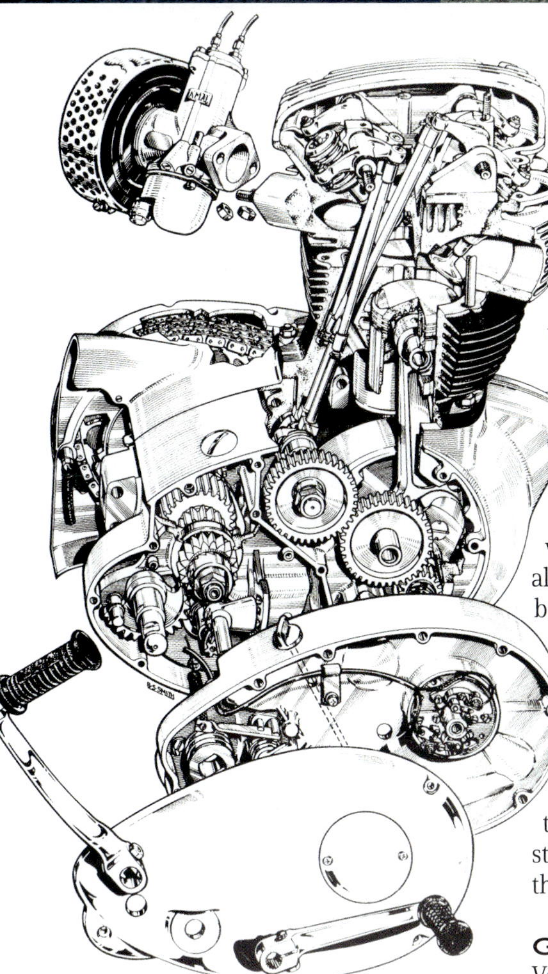

The new unit set-up also permitted shorter, beefier primary drive via duplex two-strand primary chain for the Triumph, and for BSA's A50/A65, triplex chains. The Americans had definitely been wanting this for the demands of competition, but accustomed to the smoother pre-unit twins, Shilton's perception of increased harshness was unshakeable.

Meriden tester, service man and then renowned Triumph restorer, the late Hughie Hancox, felt the same way, but wrote about the subject more thoughtfully. "The problems with the larger (650 unit) twins were all down to rigidity. The earlier pre-unit bikes did vibrate but it was liveable with due to the bikes' overall flexibility. Having separate engine, gearbox and transmission, a lot more give – and indeed forgiveness – was apparent, but with the unit construction 650 engine, and even the later 750 twins where the complete engine was a stressed member of a very rigid frame, there was no forgiveness at all."

GOOD VIBRATIONS?

Vibration was inherent in any 360° parallel twin cylinder design like Turner's original, where the pistons move up and down together. The unit construction twins did shake more, particularly at speed, than some of their surprisingly smooth Triumph predecessors, but this was most apparent to riders who had experienced both. To young Americans the shakes could even be part of the unit twins' charm, their character. It's worth remembering that even recently, the successful

Shilton believed that it was American demand for a smoother looking engine which had led to the gearbox being built in unit with the engine. He acknowledged that it did eliminate the tiresomely time-consuming job of adjusting a pre-unit's primary chain by loosening off the gearbox, moving it backward, and finally having to re-tighten the rear chain.

Harley-Davidson Evo V-twins, despite their rubber-mounted engines, had a carefully calculated amount of vibration engineered into them, to convey that macho 'real machine' flavour.

With the 1960s unit twins, it could be a bit rawer. One UK early unit Bonneville owner reported needing five new batteries in four years. Also, three rectifiers, two alternators and 19 ammeters, which the vibrations had sent open-circuit. And that's not even mentioning blown bulbs. If you wanted to ride fast and far, highly tuned unit parallel twin shakes could be more than an irritation. "Who could cruise fast on an A65 Spitfire?" asked hard-riding journalist Dave Minton. Back in the day he'd run one on test from Essex to Norfolk, with some Germans on BMWs, leading them all the way, but riding "a clanking ruin into my garage." Next day Minton had to visit his doctor suffering from 'Wimpey Fist', a common complaint among workmen using road drills – inflamed tendons due to excessive vibration.

Yet the 1960's kids didn't seem to mind. This was part of the decade's transformation of motorcycling from primary transport to leisure activity. With a younger demographic for owners, riding two-wheelers on a daily commute or on long journeys became rarer. America's *Cycle World* in 1969 identified the typical Bonneville rider as "a short-haul sort of a guy who slicks his hair back and 'gasses it' incessantly." With a 115mph top speed on test, vibration was not going to be a greaser's primary consideration.

The Great
ALL-ROUNDER

IF ONE MODEL MARKED BSA'S APEX IT WAS THE LEGENDARY GOLD STAR. A FOUR-STROKE SINGLE THAT DEFINED A GENERATION.

BSA's Gold Star was a high point in the marque's achievements. Despite its pre-war origins, it was a charismatic, powerful-looking machine. And thanks to being competition-bred and continuously developed, it really delivered.

By the start of the 1960s its days were numbered. Even in the mid-1950s, Bert Hopwood, heading a talented team of its development engineers, considered it old-fashioned. But its fate was sealed when Triumph's Edward Turner became head of BSA's new Automotive Division in 1957.

According to BSA's David Munro, Turner (correctly) perceived the Gold Star single as a threat to his sports 500, the Tiger 100 twin, which Goldies had trounced at the Clubman's TT. Gold Star development ended abruptly from that point. Lucas winding down production of the magneto was used as a further excuse when the end approached in the early 1960s.

Though the 350cc version had been made to special order only from 1957, and the 500cc only in scrambles and Clubmans racing variants, the final DBD34 continued to be produced until the beginning of 1963. Rumour had it that some American dealers refused to take their quota of BSA twins unless it included some Gold Stars.

The Clubmans came with a stern warning that it "was neither intended nor suitable for road use as a touring motorcycle." But a new shop in Banbury run by Captain Eddie Dow, winner of the 1955 Senior Clubman's TT on a Gold Star, did excellent business with young leather jacketed customers, selling both Clubmans Gold Stars, and associated goodies like his 'Duetto' TLS front brake, 'Superleggera' double-damped front fork internals, racing seats and five-gallon fibreglass petrol tanks. Dow's mechanic John Gleed described how at the end of a Saturday, the pavement outside the

BELOW *The top twin. A 1962/63 A10 Rocket Gold Star slotted a 650cc Super Rocket engine into Goldie cycle parts.*

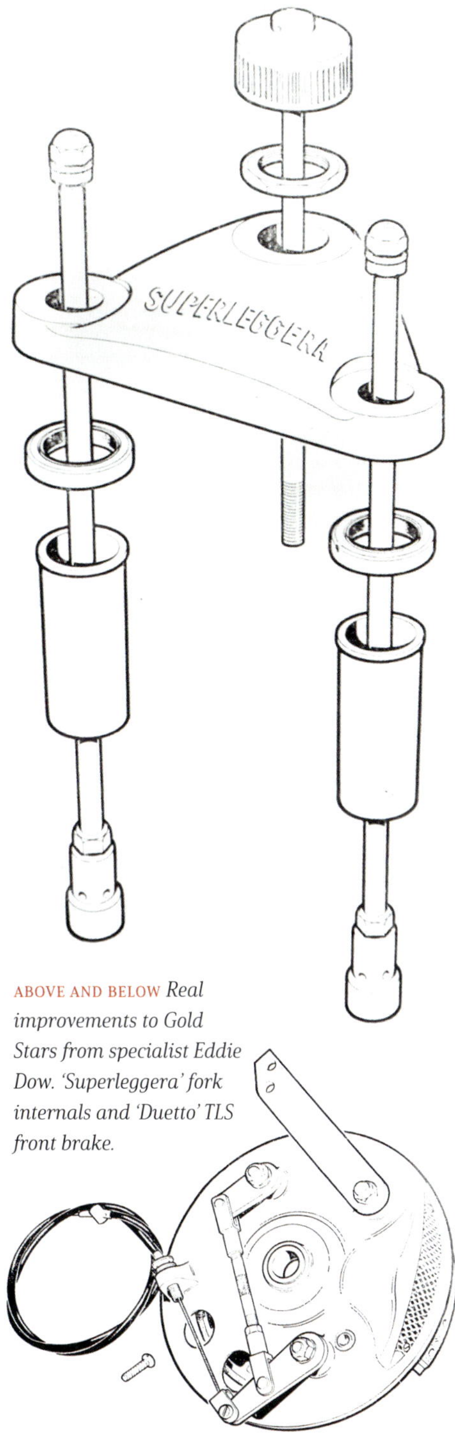

ABOVE AND BELOW *Real improvements to Gold Stars from specialist Eddie Dow. 'Superleggera' fork internals and 'Duetto' TLS front brake.*

BELOW *Empty country roads favoured the final DBD34 Clubmans 500 Gold Star.*

shop would be littered with discarded steel tanks, seats and other original parts. Rockers weren't interested in 'touring.'

A HARD MASTER

But it was true that the big Gold Stars were not the easiest of machines to live with. For openers, they could be difficult to start. You needed a good magneto; the carburation, particularly on the Clubmans' Amal GP, had to be set up right; and you had to know the correct starting drill. This culminated with what one owner called giving the kickstart "a

good welt. A lot of people aren't aggressive enough with them." It was the normal big single drill, on steroids. Starting a hot engine could be even harder. In a street race it would often be simpler to push and bump-start them. But by the time you'd done that, the opposition on famously easy-starting Triumph twins would be in the next county.

The GP lacked a reliable tickover setting, so revs had to be kept at a healthy level, above 3,000 rpm, which in traffic meant blipping the throttle constantly, to avoid stalling and a hot start. Gearing in the famously close ratio RRT2 box included a first gear so high that the clutch had to be slipped until beyond 30mph. The reward was that you could then accelerate hard in first gear all the way up to 65mph! But the BSA six-spring clutch, prone to clutch slip, got used up quickly and reacted badly if it was slipped much in traffic.

Also, as Eddie Dow later admitted, "under normal roadgoing conditions (often) the Gold Star owner couldn't cope with the 'cammy' characteristic of the engine," which though ohv, featured real power only coming in at about 3,500 rpm, with quite a sharp step. This was due to the large amount of valve overlap. As contemporary Gold Star guru Phil Pearson put it, "with a Gold Star, there's

no enjoyment in going slow. If you're going to have a Gold Star, you're going to have to *ride*".

So why do it? Because the race-bred DBD34 would maintain high speed for long durations without signs of stress. Top end on a production version was 110mph, and the 500cc version was a remarkably durable machine at speed, as long as it was ridden correctly i.e. keeping a sharp eye on the tachometer and the 6,800 rev limit. The Goldie's Achilles heel in racing, due to being developed from a production roadster, was its three-piece, built-up crankshaft. This featured many holes and rivets, all potential stress points. But away from a race-track, it was not liable to give trouble.

ORIGINS

In 1937 Bert Perrigo and others had worked on BSA's flagship Empire Star 500 to create a one-off sports bike with an alloy top end. Racer Wal Handley was persuaded out of retirement, and racing the special BSA at Brooklands' banked track, lapped at 107.47 mph. This ton-plus lap qualified for a Brooklands Gold Star. A slower M24 Gold Star was produced for 1938, but the real link to the post-war Goldie was Val Page's 1939/40 B29 350. Engines that survived the war became the basis of 1949's ZB32.

ABOVE *BSA works rider Arthur Lampkin on a scrambles Gold Star.*

ABOVE RIGHT *The Clubmans' massive downdraught 1 ½ inch Amal GP track carb was fiddly for road use, but part of the power package.*

RIGHT *The US West Coast version of the 500 Gold Star.*

The first Gold Stars were all 350cc versions, with the secret weapon in their development being the great Irish all-round rider Bill Nicholson. A successful works trials and scrambles rider, in the light of his experience he built his own duplex downtube cradle frame for 1951. Having already associated with fellow Irishmen the McCandless brothers, who designed Norton's Featherbed frame, he then added swinging-arm rear suspension for his scrambler, and persuaded BSA managing director James Leek to accept it for production. The 1953 Gold Stars were the first BSAs with an all-welded swinging-arm frame, which became the basis of the pre-unit singles', and of all the twins' chassis until 1970. The Gold Star gearbox to suit this frame, based on Hopwood's design for his A7/A10 twins, with its short shafts was the strongest available.

The 350cc won the Junior Clubman's TT in 1949 and 500cc ZB34s took Gold in the 1951 ISDT and from then on. By 1954 the 500cc won the Senior Clubman's TT. After the following year, Gold Star dominance led to the Clubman's TT being discontinued on the Island.

In 1954, with the popularity of trials on the wane, innovative development swung from the 350cc to the 500cc version. James Leek decided that BSA should now fully contest scrambles and production racing. Hopwood persuaded Leek that the 500cc

should have the massive square-finned head and barrel already agreed upon for the 350. Development wizard Roland Pike wrote that the resulting CB Series Gold Star for April 1954 was "almost a new engine." It was in scrambles, incidentally, rather than on tarmac, with works riders like John Draper and Jeff Smith, that the Goldie successfully competed at Grand Prix level.

SMALL HEATH'S FINEST

Hopwood's special A7 twins dominated that year's Daytona Beach 200 race, though a Gold Star with a special hard-tail frame came third. In 1956, 500cc Goldies were second, third, fourth and fifth behind an all-conquering Harley KR 750cc side-valve which the AMA rules allowed, and again were second and third in 1957. The leading BSA riders had all come from California. There, West Coast BSA boss Hap Alzina had fought the AMA to get BSA accepted at Daytona. He also presided over further tuning of both Small Heath's singles and twins, including the use of W & S valve springs. Chuck Minnert on a Gold Star won the

Catalina Island GP race in 1956, and BSA scramblers in the US were known as the Catalina after that.

BSA World Champion scrambler Jeff Smith said later that "My favourite race bike of all time was the works Gold Star. It was big and heavy, but it was so easy to ride. It had what I call a happy engine – it never felt over-stressed."

Early Gold Stars had been individually assembled by two-man teams, from selected parts. This careful assembly remained for works machines when the stock machines were assembled on the line as production rose, but never to more than 2,000 a year. Each one came with a Certificate of Performance after being dynamometer-tested for power. The Goldie offered many different engine and trim options – pistons from 6.5:1 to 9.0:1, and higher, compression, three different gearbox ratios etc – emphasizing and enhancing the machine's versatility.

BSA's metallurgy was then second to none. They made their own pistons, and

RIGHT *"You're going to have to ride."*

BELOW RIGHT *This is the Gold Star Clubmans rider's-eye view. The rev counter was important.*

Gold Star examples were machined with an industrial diamond for a mirror-like finish. Flywheels were polished, as was the crankcase, the inlet port and the forged con rods. The latter were produced at Small Heath's forge, and Pike wrote that "I believe the forged steel con rods…were outstandingly good." The high quality metallurgy also benefitted the austenitic iron which lined the alloy barrel, the piston rings, and the Nimonic 80 valve material. BSA's own carbo-nitriding hardening process strengthened the camshafts, in contrast to Triumph twins' problems in that area. The Gold Star represented the sum of everything that was good about Small Heath.

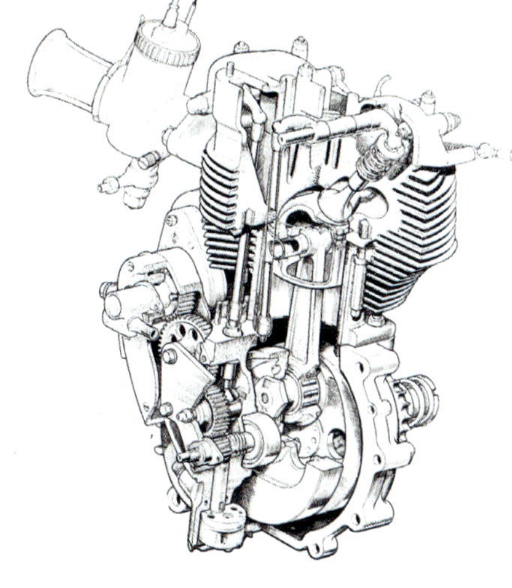

ABOVE *The classic Gold Star engine.*

LEFT *The DBD34's slim tall profile, with long fork stanchions dictated by high steering head.*

The DBD34 also looked the business. Tall and imposing, black cycle parts were topped by the chromed petrol tank. In contrast, Edward Turner had abandoned Triumph's chromed tanks, leaving the 'jewellery' to metallic badges and styling strips. The Goldie's tank featured a butterfly filler cap, and maroon-lined frosted-silver panels bearing the iconic five-inch round plastic badges. Slender mudguards were chromed, like the rear chainguard and brake back plates. The Clubmans' twinned instruments and factory-fitted dropped 'clip-on' handlebars were the cherries on the cake.

None of this came cheap. In 1960 a DBD34 would set you back £307, against a Triumph T120 Bonneville at £284.

ON THE ROAD

If you could master the difficulty of starting it, the DBD34, weighing in at 365lb, with its excellent frame was easy to ride. The front brake was either BSA's eight-inch SLS stopper which if set up right was excellent of its kind, or the optional 190mm type, which had been a compromise between road work and scrambling, with a diameter of just under 7 ½in.

Standard BSA forks with rebound-only damping and a characteristic clang on full extension, could bottom out interestingly on bumpy bends at speed. The Superleggera or similar double-damped conversion was worthwhile. The exhaust, with its 1957-on swept-back pipe increasing cornering clearance, gave a very loud, flat roar. Only a silencer with not just the external shape but the correct internals, which caused a characteristic 'twitter' on the over-run, would release the Goldie's power.

On a clear road, once you got past the clutch-slipping, and the wind of speed had taken the strain off your wrists from the clip-ons, at 70mph in top the engine was hardly working at all. And you were at the bottom of an endless, and endlessly steepening power curve. This unstoppable feeling of power accumulating with each detonation and carrying you on and on further up the scale than most, defined the Goldie as the ultimate ohv single. It did take its time to get to ton-plus speeds in top. There were hard shakes through the Goldie's dropped bars from 3,500 to 4,000 rpm, and overtaking, you didn't whip round cars as you would on a twin but hammered your way past.

If this bike were a county, it would have been Yorkshire. Gritty, uncompromisingly masculine, no-nonsense; it delivered, and went on delivering, in a crunch. You can see why the minority who chose them often found that, after a Goldie, nothing else would do.

Ingenious
TWO-STROKE 250

THE EARLS COURT CYCLE AND MOTORCYCLE SHOW IN NOVEMBER 1958 WAS A PIVOTAL MOMENT IN TWO-WHEELED TRANSPORT. IT WAS BILLED AS 'THE SHOW WHERE THE SCOOTER AND MOTORCYCLE FINALLY MET'.

In the 1950s Italian scooters had been a genuine phenomenon in Britain, a transport revolution. By then, along with mopeds, they were outselling motorcycles in the UK. They were light, un-menacing, cheerful, weather-proof, with zippy two-stroke engines covered in brightly coloured panelling. And their open frames made them popular with riders in skirts, which opened up a fresh 50% of a new market.

The 1958 show concentrated on British ride-to-work relative lightweights, with degrees of enclosure, weather protection, and colour, for youngsters and women. There was the previous year's Triumph rear-enclosed 350cc 'Twenty-One', and its new imitator the Norton 250cc Jubilee twin. There were BSA/Triumph's new Sunbeam and Tigress scooters. But above all, there was the genuinely revolutionary Ariel Leader.

ENTER 'GILDA'

Since 1955, under new general manager Ken Whistance, Ariel had been looking for a fresh direction. The company was known for their traditional, quality big singles, twins, and the flagship 1,000cc Square Four. Canvassing dealers indicated that for the majority middle-to-lightweight market, a 250cc two-stroke twin, like the many European examples, would be the way forward. Visiting foreign shows convinced Whistance that expensive tubular frames were out, and that for economy, pressure die-casting of the engine parts was essential. Ariel's project was to be named 'Gilda'.

For this, his final design before retiring in 1959, the brilliant Val Page was assisted by the younger Bernard Knight. The engine selected bore a close resemblance to 1955's two-stroke twin, the German Adler (Eagle) MB 250S, with its separate cylinders inclined forward at 45 degrees. Their pistons were even interchangeable. Whether there was more to it than 'careful study' has never become known.

ABOVE *Ancient and modern. A wartime Ariel W/NG ohv 350 single (Right) with an Ariel Leader twin, launched 13 years after war's end.*

ABOVE *The Leader arrives for 1959.*

Page was admired for his production economy, and certainly modified the basic Adler design along those lines. Where the expensive Adler's two crankshaft flywheel assemblies had been gear-coupled, on the Leader they featured mating taper ends secured simply by a captive bolt. Adler ceased motorcycle production in 1957. When the Leader was launched late in 1958, a German newspaper headlined 'The Eagle has landed in Birmingham'!

In Page's design, the engine and its four-speed gearbox in a separate but unified shell, was mounted below a deep beam box-like structure of welded steel pressings. This was very rigid and ensured excellent handling. Front suspension was unusual, featuring a trailing-link set-up, which eliminated nose-dive during heavy braking. The frame beam was topped by a dummy fuel tank, with the real one beneath the hinged dual seat, contributing to a low centre of gravity.

Between the forks sat a full-width hub brake, alloy at first, of six inch diameter, with the rear one similar. To keep saddle height down, the Ariel rode on quickly-detachable 16 x 3.25 wheels, with whitewall tyres. A strange aspect to the ride was that, due to the fork's lack of a top yoke, the handlebars were mounted on the central steering column. This meant that when cornering, the bars moved while the bodywork stayed put.

CLEVER STUFF

This sound, basic design was supplemented by many ingenious features. The dummy tank contained a parcel compartment big enough to take a peakless helmet, as well as the steering lock and the seat catch. A neat lever on the instrument panel altered the setting of the headlamp in its cowl. The control cables were concealed and protected, scooter-style, beneath a pressed-steel cover on the handlebars.

ABOVE *An Ariel Arrow from 1961.*

Unusually for the time, the stop-light was operated by both the front and rear brakes. A range of extras was offered, including an eight-day clock which replaced an existing Ariel badge on the panel. A fold-out lifting handle helped get the fully kitted out 330lb Leader onto its centre stand. A windshield was fitted as standard, and its angle could be altered to suit (some) riders' heights.

The extras were beguiling, especially to obsessives who had to have them all. They include colour-coordinated panniers and their fitted inners, a rear carrier with straps, additional springs for the rear units to stiffen up handling if a passenger and luggage was carried, and later, a chromed rear bumper bar. The display light for the direction indicators, a useful first on a British bike, doubled as a neutral light.

The Leader was soft-tuned, with the 8.2:1 compression giving 16bhp @ 6,400rpm. On test, top speed was limited to 67mph, when anything less than 70 was unlikely to impress young riders. The Vincent Owners Club speculated whether the eight-day clock was to help time

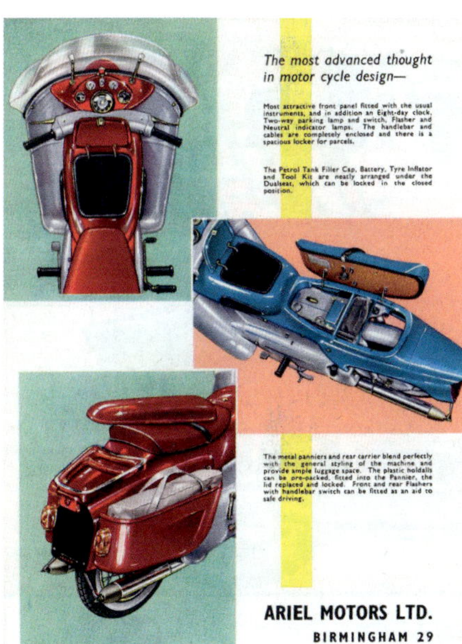

ABOVE *Details of Leader's equipment and extras revealed.*

LEFT *A fully equipped Leader.*

the Leader's unimpressive performance over a standing ¼ mile! The Ariel turned into a 'Marmite' machine, initially quite successful among those who bought into the whole package, but scorned by some as 'the Bleader' or 'The Tin Hippopotamus'.

Launched at £209, against £195 for a Vespa GS and £228 for a Triumph 'Twenty-One', by 1960 the price had dropped to £197 as the home market began to contract. With the US

LEADER
data

Engine: Twin cylinder, two-stroke
Bore and stroke: 54 × 54 mm. (2⅛″ × 2⅛″)
Capacity: 247 c.c. (15 cu. in.)
Compression ratio: 10:1
Engine b.h.p.: 17.5
Engine r.p.m.: 7,000
Gear ratio, top: 5.9
Gear ratio, third: 7.8
Gear ratio, second: 11
Gear ratio, first: 19
Engine revs. top gear: 1,000 = 11 m.p.h. (18 km.h.)

Tyre, front: Ribbed, white wall, 16″ × 3.25″
Tyre, rear: Studded, white wall, 16″ × 3.25″
Wheelbase: 51″ (130 cm.)
Overall length: 77″ (195.5 cm.)
Overall width: 27″ (68.5 cm.)
Dualseat height: 30″ (76 cm.)
Ground clearance: 5″ (12.5 cm.)
Weight (standard specification): 320 lb. (145 kg.)
Petrol tank capacity: 3 gallons, reserve ½ gallon (13½ litres)
Approximate petrol consumption: 80 m.p.g. (28 km.p.l.)
Approximate maximum speed: 70 m.p.h. (113 km.h.)

Note: Speed and petrol consumption figures apply to machines that have been run in for 1,000 miles (1.600 km.).

Petrol consumption figures are based on a steady speed of 40 m.p.h. (65 km.h.).

ABOVE *A cheerful Leader rider (though probably damp around the edges) in this promotional flyer. The specs are for the later post-1961 machine.*

ABOVE RIGHT *There were few takers for 1964's underpowered, economy Arrow 200.*

RIGHT *The Arrow Super Sports, a.k.a. the Golden Arrow.*

uninterested in panelled models, domestic sales were vital. They were not helped as the ever-conservative British motorcycling public learned about some of the Hippopotamus' drawbacks.

DOWNSIDES

Cold-starting the Leader could be difficult, due to the absenc e of a lever through a slit in the panelling to tickle the 7/8in carburettor, as featured on the Jubilee. The butterfly choke could also be tricky to set right, even after a notch had been cut in it to give a half-way setting. An electric start would have been the answer, as offered optionally on the Sunbeam/Tigress scooters, but once again the various parts of the BSA Group empire were not communicating.

On the move, comfort was good, handling excellent, and 60mph cruising a reality. But the only 16 inch tyre available had been a particularly non-sticky Dunlop, which severely compromised roadholding in the rain. The gearchange from the slimmed-down Burman CP box's internals was slow and crunchy, especially changing down. Its ratios were ill-chosen too, first being so low as to be virtually unusable. Even with a possible 80mpg, the small, 2¼ gallon petrol tank limited range.

But the most striking failure were the brakes, dismissed as 'appallingly feeble' by motorcycling guru L.J.K. Setright. A braking figure of 30ft or lower at 30mph was the average for most motorcycles on test. The Leader's figure was 36ft, although with a later, lighter variant, the Sports Arrow, Motor Cycling magazine managed to get that down to 34 ½ feet. No development would improve the brakes, which could not be enlarged due to the fork design.

Of the scooter features, clearly no one in a skirt was going to straddle the Leader's 31in seat height and being some 80lb heavier than a Lambretta didn't help. The weather protection wasn't quite perfect, either. You were supposed to be able to ride in normal clothing and footwear, one of a scooter's attractions. But in a raincoat and shoes as advised, in the rain your shoulders with the low, narrow screen, got wet. So did your gloved hands due to the screens limited hand-blisters, while your shoes filled up with water.

While undoing a single catch removed the panelling over a Vespa's engine, the Leader's panels were held on by five screws on each side, and not quick-release Dzus fasteners either. And to remove the right side panel, the kickstart and gear lever had to be unbolted as well. Riders, ever the final development engineers, learned to use bits of rubber with the screws to stop the panels drumming.

FASTER

The Leader was a bit too utilitarian, and sales fell off. Things picked up when Edward Turner's sense of a market that was now increasingly youth-oriented, kicked in. Though Whistance was reportedly unenthusiastic, a stripped Leader covered in plasticine mouldings was spotted in the Meriden office of Jack Wickes, Turner's 'pencil'.

The result for 1960 was the Arrow, its seat height dropped to 28½in and the dummy tank re-shaped like a racing pannier one. 'Ears' at the front of it supported a disproportionately small-looking six-inch headlamp. The Arrow was not a thing of beauty, but the price dropped to £167 and the weight to 275lb. Output and top speed were raised to 17.5bhp and over 70mph.

This did the trick, and sales rose, with 1,600 two-strokes produced in a single week. Turner used the sales successes as an excuse to terminate the Ariel four-strokes. The Arrow proved a good basis for tuning. It began to do well in sprints. In the 1960 Lightweight TT, a Hermann Meier-tuned version putting out 26bhp came a creditable seventh ahead of some exotic Italian competition.

In mid-1961, what the leather boys had really wanted came along, with the Super Sports variant, known as the Golden Arrow due to its striking polychromatic

ABOVE *Tuned Ariel Arrows formed the basis of successful sprinters and racers.*

Gold and Ivory finish, with extra chrome. All engines were now 10:1 compression ratio, providing the Sports with a 20bhp output, thanks to cylinder heads redesigned with squish-type chambers and an axial spark plug position.

For 1961 the petrol tank was enlarged to three gallons. The Golden Arrow, with altered gearing and a 1 1/16 inch carburettor, was good for 75mph, though still just pipped by Royal Enfield's Sports Continental. With 'ace' dropped handlebars featuring red grips, it handled well, though limited by the centre-stand grounding, as well as by pitching and weaving above 60mph. With the dropped bars the footrests were too far forward, but with excellent, responsive acceleration if you kept it up in the rev band, you could forget that.

Golden Arrows were the ones to have, often seen and heard yowling around town, invariably trailing thick smoke. Two-stroke oil technology was changing, and if you put oils with additives in at the 24:1 ratio recommended for those without, your Arrow's rear end finished up even more oil-splattered. By the end Ariel was advising a 32:1 ratio.

By 1963 the home market collapse was really biting, and with just 15 orders on the books, Ariel's Selly Oak home was closed down. Two-stroke production was moved in with BSA at Small Heath. For May 1964 the standard Arrow was dropped in favour of the £10 cheaper Arrow 200, its bore sleeved down to 48.5mm, to take advantage of cheaper insurance. But at 14bhp it was a poor thing, and only 1,000 or so sold before the end arrived in mid-1965, hastened by Burman ceasing motorcycle gear production.

The Leader had been an interesting experiment, with 21,800 produced, representing about half of the respectable 42,000 total of Ariel two-strokes. It had been let down by penny-pinching, with poor paint finish and the lack of undercoating on its concealed portions, plus the bad state of British alternator electrics. Home mechanic jobs like changing a throttle cable or adjusting the carburettor were tricky. And the engine could occasionally seize if the carburettor settings were wrong, though in general it was a reliable unit. But by the mid-Sixties, Gilda's day was done.

ABOVE *Famous Trials rider Olga Kevelos production racing a Golden Arrow at the Thruxton 500 in 1962.*

Two-wheel TEARAWAYS

BANK HOLIDAYS AND RIDES TO THE SEASIDE MEANT TWO VERY DIFFERENT THINGS TO 1960S FAMILIES AND 1960S BIKERS.

ABOVE *Banned in UK until 1968, the movie The Wild One was influencing Rockers long before that.*

RIGHT *A pre-unit BSA twin fan outside the Ace.*

In post-war Britain, even when austerity and rationing began to lift, the prolonged sacrifices and self-control of World War Two meant that any kind of extravagance or unconventional behaviour was strongly disapproved of. Vehicles were dull-coloured and slow, and a stifling respectability covered suburban Metroland.

So, of course that had to be rebelled against by young baby-boomers. And with reasonable wages and low inflation, they had money to spend to help them do it. By 1959, five million newly minted UK teenagers had a disposable annual income of £800 million.

REBEL, REBEL
This relative prosperity meant that one of the vanguard rebel tribes, the Rockers, could not just afford to buy fast motorbikes on the HP. (Although to keep themselves in petrol and spares,

they often couldn't smoke or drink.) They could also try to make their bikes even faster, with tuning goodies and racing accessories – speed was king and their heroes were racers. With machines made as individual as the leather jackets they decorated with studs, cloth patches, metal pins and paint, the bikes went beyond transport to become status symbols, an expression of individuality, of identity.

The older generation were used to obeying and being obeyed, and the Rockers' defiance of authority caused resentment and outrage. The competition-bred machines they favoured were mainly

twins from Triumph, BSA and Norton – in the early 1960s Britain was producing the fastest street motorcycles in the world. And Rockers persisted with British bikes until the end of the 1960s – 'Rebels Don't Ride Japanese'.

Being fast, large, noisy and oily, their motorcycles, and by extension, others too, were perceived by the public as a dangerous nuisance. And this dislike of two-wheelers' new image extended to politicians. Parliament persistently blocked legislation to make the use of mopeds

ABOVE *Paul Dunstall was a premier Triton builder and Rocker influencer.*

cheap and unlicensed, as it was in Europe, which could have helped our industry.

TOO FAST TO LIVE, TOO YOUNG TO DIE
Parents thought that the Rockers' Brylcreemed pompadours, white silk scarves and leather gear were both effeminate and menacing, with echoes of the old SS black and silver – a double result in boys' age-old struggle to differentiate themselves from their fathers.

The end of the two year period of National Service for 17 to 21-year-olds, from November 1960, added another element to youth's perceived indiscipline. Rockers were almost exclusively working class boys and a few girls, with the odd bohemian outriders, students and artists. The monotony and frustration of day-long factory work pushed young men on motorcycles to get together. Not in the trending coffee bars with their Gaggia machines and glass cups, but in transport cafes with the sugar spoon chained to the counter, where noise and leather gear were not a problem. The juke boxes played new rock and roll, from Elvis to Little Richard. Rockers weren't called Rockers because of their valve gear, though it was a happy ambivalence.

There were biker-friendly transport cafes dotted around the country, but the centre was London and the epicentre the Ace Café on the old North Circular Road beyond Hanger Lane. Once a humble shack, after bomb damage, by 1951 it had been transformed with neon signage, glass frontage and a clock tower. There were petrol pumps, a separate shirt-and-tie restaurant and upstairs rooms for the long-distance lorry drivers, and one of the UK's first automatic car washes. As the end of the core café racer/ coffee bar cowboy era approached in 1962, up to 1,000 motorcycles would visit the Ace in a single evening.

The Ace was unusual in staying open 24 hours a day. So, when cafes like the Dug-Out in Golders Green or the Cellar in Windsor turned out, Rockers there would ride and race to the Ace. It was the same when the Soho coffee bars shut for the night. Music people like the diminutive singer Adam Faith, on a Bonneville with cut-down rear shocks to lower its height, and the producer Mickie Most, headed for the all-night cafe.

ABOVE *Two Rockers outside the Ace Café.*

RIGHT *"Suicide Club" - the story that changed things for Rockers.*

At the Ace in this era there was an instinctive hierarchy. Top riders like 'King of the Ace' Barry 'Noddy' Chase, and specials builder Ron Witchell, sat at the two tables nearest the entrance, with their bikes parked nearest to the door outside. Newcomers who parked further away might emerge to find bits from their bikes, or the bikes themselves, missing.

Witchell went on to production race for Gus Kuhn, before his death on the track in 1972. Other Ace graduates who became professional racers included Dave Degens, several times Barcelona winner and founder of Dresda Autos of Triton fame; Ray Pickrell, top BSA/Triumph rider and TT winner on the triples; and Dave 'Crasher' Croxford of the works NVT Commando team. These were some seriously fast boys.

The elite were week-night regulars, not drop-ins, or part of the Thursday night crowd when Wembley speedway with its 85,000 fans was over. At the Ace there were larks, like chaining the juke-box to a departing lorry, but surprisingly little violence.

DEMON TWEAKS

Most of the fast riders were engineering apprentices or garage mechanics. British bikes were both high maintenance, and simple enough to work on if you had the skills. With money lacking for professional mechanics even if you could find a trustworthy one, Rockers mostly did their own spannering or adaptations. There were inevitably some bodgers, but many were competent mechanically and some highly skilled.

Building up a café racer might involve fitting clip-on or ace handlebars. Skinny alloy mudguards might be chosen, with front fork springs either exposed or rubber-gaitered. Large race-style petrol tanks in alloy or fibreglass were favoured as were racing seats, or at least leopard-skin patterned covers for the originals. 'Bacon-slicer' cooling discs could embellish the front brake. Despite most of the action taking place after dark, headlights might be stripped off for the racer look, with just a bicycle lamp fitted to satisfy the law. Swept-back exhaust pipes, sometimes siamesed, might lead to megaphone silencers, or ones with no internals.

The ultimate adaptation was the Triton, with the fast, tuneable Triumph engine married to the superior Norton Featherbed frame. The pre-unit Triumph engines were favoured for easier chain-lines, and the older Wideline Norton chassis. Soon Dresda and others would be providing the necessary ancillaries.

On engines, the cheapness and availability of performance parts was one reason why Triumphs became the thing, despite the pre-units' poor handling. From about 1955, with the sports T110 650, they became the most popular Rocker mount, though the more robust BSAs also had their following. Nortons were admired for their handling, but with less than 10,000 machines overall produced a year, they were scarcer and more expensive.

And neither Norton or BSA offered, until 1962 and 1965 respectively, the ultimate go-faster look accessory, twin carburettors. Triumph had supplied

ABOVE *Triumphs were the thing. And nuclear disarmament?*

ABOVE *A 'Suicide Club' rider's 700cc Royal Enfield Constellation outside the Ace today.*

these in speed kits for the pre-unit T100 and T110. Then for 1959 they bit the bullet with the production of the twin carb T120 Bonneville. The twin instruments might be fiddly to set up and synchronize, and they only offered marginal performance advantage. But the sight of them said, 'I'm serious about speed'.

CAFÉ SOCIETY

Other well-known Rocker venues were the Busy Bee, eight miles north of the Ace on the old Watford by-pass, and Johnson's on the A20 by Brands Hatch. Riders at all of them were burdened with drum brakes, hard tyres of non-sticky

ABOVE *Mark Wilsmore at the Ace Café he struggled so hard to revive.*

ABOVE RIGHT *Outside the Ace today.*

rubber, the British weather, poor lights and outdated roads. But the need for speed and belief in your own luck and skill trumped everything.

The Ace café racers did take their chances, usually after midnight when, before 1961, the police patrols would have gone home. There were high speed runs to the Busy Bee. But the ultimate burn-up was the 3 ½ mile round-trip run from the Ace north to the Neasden roundabout and back. This was alleged to have to be done, from a standing start, before a three minute record on the Ace's juke box had finished.

The route along the North Circular hit the treacherous Iron Bridge, with its ridge in the road which used to nearly have riders of rigid machines off. The Bridge had to be exited, stands scraping and

sparks flying, at no less than 90mph if you were to make the time. One night a rider was passed by a fast pack heading for the Busy Bee. Then in the distance he saw all their tail-lights shoot up into the air. An articulated lorry had pulled out of a side-road and they had smashed into the side of it. The injured riders survived, but two young girl pillion passengers were killed instantly. In a single fortnight, seven motorcyclists were killed at the Bridge.

THE CHANGE

With 1,680 riders killed in 1959, many of them youngsters, this could not continue. Early in 1961 an episode of TV's popular 'Dixon of Dock Green' featured record-racing. Then in February the *Daily Mirror* ran its front page 'Suicide Club' story. After that had established young Rockers as menaces to society, the next day leather boys from everywhere converged on the Ace, did too many ton-up runs past the café on the 40mph North Circular, then threw things and

jeered at motorists. This provoked a police raid that night, with 20 arrests.

Following that, things changed. Later in the year, Parliament introduced the law limiting learner riders to machines no larger than 250cc. The police were equipped with 100mph Triumph SAINT 650s and 125mph Daimler Dart pursuit cars. They began patrolling all night. There would be no upper speed limit until 1967, but conviction on police say-so for "driving at a speed dangerous to the public" meant instant loss of licence. The Ace became quieter.

The Rocker phenomenon continued countrywide, fuelled by the Mods v Rockers seaside clashes in 1964. Those were a press creation. A London council estate Mod said, "It never occurred to me to beat Rockers up; they used to help us fix our scooters." But the tribalism which the publicity whipped up lingered on in the provinces for a decade.

In London, as Roy Wittich's fast-riding widow Jenny put it: "All our group knew the risks, but I think some of the young ones coming in (to the café racing scene) in the 1960s just took chances, without calculating." The skilled, dedicated speed men moved on. The growing motorway network saw the need for transport cafes going, and the Ace itself became sleazier, with drug-dealing by the early patch clubs. As blues-based music, pot-smoking and girls liberated by the pill, saw 1960s youth dance off in another direction, the Ace closed in 1969.

But as former Rocker Barry Innes said: "A lot of people, their lives ended when the Ace closed." The persistence of Rocker spirit and nostalgia saw the cafe opened again in 2001, by rockabilly fan and former mounted policeman Mark Wilsmore. It is a much friendlier, less edgy establishment than the original.

ABOVE *A Triumph pre-unit engine in a Featherbed frame = Triton, the ultimate café racer.*

Best
OF THE BEST

NAMED AFTER THE BONNEVILLE SALT FLATS – AMERICA'S CATHEDRAL OF SPEED - A 650CC BONNIE WAS THE ONE TO HAVE.

ABOVE *The first T120 missed the 1959 catalogue, but a few of these sheets did appear.*

ABOVE *John Holder, with Tony Godfrey, proved the Bonnie wasn't just a pretty face, winning the 1962 Thruxton 500.*

"If I had to pick just one bike as the British bike of the 1960s," wrote well-known motorcycle journalist Bob Currie, "I would plump unhesitatingly for the Triumph Bonneville."

The combination of mass production plus its design and engineering flair branded the T120, the 650cc Bonnie, into the souls of more than one age group of riders, on more than one continent. The interaction of US and English dreams and achievements forged the Bonnie's inimitable style. In fact its cutting edge was often the product of tension between the two cultures.

EVOLUTION

Famously, Edward Turner had been reluctant to offer a sporting production 650 with twin carburettors. The elements had emerged in the Fifties. The splayed port twin carb cylinder head had come from the 500cc pre-unit Tiger 100, at first only as part of a race kit. In March 1958 the sports T110 650cc had gained a one-piece crankshaft to handle extra power.

As John Nelson, Triumph service manager and author of 'Bonnie', described: "Unofficially, engines had already been assembled with pistons that had strange-looking crowns, with valve springs and camshafts smuggled in from America." The camshafts included the Bonneville's famous E3134.

Turner only made up his mind about the hot 650 too late for it to be included in the 1959 catalogue. It was primarily aimed at Americans demanding higher performance. Its name came from the US, celebrating Johnny Allen's 1956 World Motorcycle Speed Record, at 214 mph in a 650cc-powered streamliner at Bonneville Salt Flats, Utah.

The first T120 was very definitely a twin carb T110. This was emphasized by styling that included Turner's famous headlamp nacelle, swept-back handlebars, a two-level dual seat, and valanced mudguards. The Turner-approved colour scheme was in a two-tone, eye-catching but hardly macho Tangerine and Pearl Grey. One Rocker remarked about the light-looking, stylish Triumph twins in general, 'They were very feminine, but all us butch bikers wanted one'.

The Americans didn't like any of that at all, and by late 1959 their variants sported a single-level dual seat, lowered, wider bars, and a Royal Blue and Pearl Grey finish. But it was 1960 that saw the real re-styling. A separate chromed headlamp allowed twinned rev-counter and speedo.

The front forks became gaitered, and painted alloy blade mudguards were fitted. The magneto remained but the dynamo was replaced by an alternator. Finish became Pearl Grey and Azure Blue. The Bonnie was emerging.

Triumph's well-known handling deficiencies at speed were addressed with a new duplex front downtube frame. This had a new three-point fixing petrol tank to suit, held down from front to rear by a chromed retaining strap. The tank being fixed directly to the frame tubes may have contributed to the frame breakages detailed in chapter three. An extra tank rail and revised tank mountings introduced mid-season cured the breakages, though they introduced more vibration.

But people loved the Bonneville, particularly for the fact that with its high speed and searing acceleration, it didn't sacrifice tractability. The 1961 T120's top speed of 110mph or more was allied to an engine that was comfortable around town at 30mph in top gear. But it could also give 50mph in first, 70mph in second, and 88 to 90mph in third, with good 'chuckability' and acceptable handling from firm suspension. The initial complex remote-float set-up for the carburettors changed to simple handed instruments.

Combined with season 1961 to 1962's peerless Silver and Sky Blue finish, the last pre-unit Bonnies, with heavier flywheels for 1962, were admirable.

UNIT

In 1963 there were improvements right away from Doug Hele's work, as the 650cc engine, cleverly restyled to maintain continuity, shifted to unit construction. The frame reverted to a single front downtube, significantly thicker for strength, retaining the 65° steering head angle. And at that frame's rear, the prime cause of Triumph twins' 'Instant Whip' was eliminated.

A brazed-in forged lug carried a new swinging-arm pivot. This lug had each of its ends secured to the rear mounting plates, which in turn were now bolted to the sub-frame. With the fork thus properly braced, and the swinging-arm itself also of stiffer construction, the handling was judged "miles better" by one young owner, compared to his previous '62 Bonnie.

The new engine's nine-stud cylinder head cured a previous problem of cracking heads. These benefits offset the adoption of troublesome alternator electrics, which John Nelson called 'a

really retrograde step'. The new engine's duplex primary drive chain was welcomed for US competition, as was its lightened, strengthened crankshaft. The first full-on T120C US racers were produced, the following year named 'the Bonneville TT' after winning the US-style TT championship in California.

For 1964 Hele offered new, sturdier, better damped, 'outside spring' front forks. After that a Motor Cycle Mechanics test judged that the Bonneville 'handled like a dream', in the wet or dry. Once again it was flexible as ever. "A Tarzan in City suiting," as Bob Currie put it. And it was easy enough to kickstart despite its 8.5:1 compression ratio. A consistent 14.6s standing quarter kept the Americans happy, and in 1964, a 115mph top speed impressed everyone. The rise in power from 46 to 47 bhp was partly thanks to bigger valves of Nimonic material, and to larger 1 1/8 in 389 carbs, now linked by an induction balance pipe.

Bonnevilles still vibrated at speed and still leaked oil, due to vertically split crankcases, to the pushrod tube design, and to thin joint faces from Triumph's 'minimum of metal' policy. The latter meant a kerbside

weight of 399lb which was 16lb lighter than their BSA A65 equivalents. 1964's Gold and Alaskan White finish was nice, but 1965's Silver and Pacific Blue was another classic.

The Bonneville's gains for 1965 included re-styled, swept-back exhausts, leading on UK models to the old, longer 'Resonator' silencers, but for the US to shorter 'teardrop' ones, 'the classic sports muffler'. To counter what was known as the rogue spark and pre-ignition leading to holed piston crowns, caused by the 4CA points, facilities for stroboscopic timing, to accurately measure TDC, were built into the engine.

TOO HOT

For 1966 the 1950s-style 'mouth-organ' tank badges were changed to the sleeker 'eye-brow' design, and mounted on slimmer US and UK gas tanks. These sat above a controversial version of the T120 engine, with the same camshafts, cam followers, larger 1 3/16in carbs and 9.5:1 compression ratio as the TT version. Speed men like Bob Innes liked it, but John Nelson judged the power characteristics of the 1966 version "more brittle than before, and much more than many road-

RIGHT *In 1961 we saw the real Bonnie emerge.*

going riders came to care for…a disguised production racer."

Output was now 48bhp at 6,700 rpm, with even more spectacular throttle response. The increased power was coped with by the fitting of an effective drive side roller main bearing. Narrow flywheels became 2 ½ lbs lighter, but vibration periods increased above 5,000 rpm, enough to split petrol tanks.

ABOVE *The 1961 T120 went as well as it looked.*

ABOVE *The 1963 Bonneville, the first unit T120, had much improved handling thanks to Hele.*

ABOVE *A 1959 'Tangerine Dream' Bonneville outside London Triumph specialists Ace Classics. The colour scheme distracted from its T110 origins.*

ABOVE *Alternative 1959 Bonneville colour scheme from mid-season for the Americans and later the Brits.*

ABOVE *With stronger, redesigned front forks, 1964 Bonneville.*

New rubber-mounted six-pint oil tanks were introduced. The US models got stainless steel mudguards until 1969. The electrics became 12 volt which finally allowed more satisfactory Zener diode voltage control, once it had been mounted in a cooling breeze for 1968. Handling was improved again. Hele steepened the steering head angle to 62° by shortening the top frame tube. This maintained the wheelbase, while putting the engine lower and further forward, giving a lower centre of gravity plus reduced front-end lightness. 'Cycle' magazine judged that the new set-up provided much improved handling and 'roadability'.

For the 1967 Bonneville, with Sturgeon's production push at full strength, there was what authors Brooke and Gaylin called 'wild quality variation'. A move to Hepolite rather than Meriden-made pistons brought holed piston tops due to initial crown thickness problems. Power on the T120 rose again as it adopted the E3134 cam for the inlet as well as the exhaust. In mid-year more modern Amal Concentric carburettors were adopted. The alternator stator became more durable with encapsulated windings. And 1967's appropriately psychedelic deep purple Aubergine and Alaskan White finish was handsome.

GLORY DAYS

The unit Bonneville's finest hours began in 1968. A new, race-derived eight-inch TLS front brake raised stopping power to a truly satisfactory level, after a problem with its cable run had been sorted mid-year. The contact breakers changed to the 6CA type with independent adjustment per cylinder and remotely mounted condensers. The front forks gained both increased travel and true two-way damping, via Hele-designed floating shuttle-valves. The Bonnie could now be laid over safely on the bumpiest of bends. In the middle of the year a final handling tweak came, with a new, longer swinging-arm of thicker section, with heavier corner fillets for added stiffness.

And 1969 saw virtually the final flowering. Looks were enhanced by exposed chrome springs on the Girling rear shocks. The 'eye-brow' tank badges were replaced by simpler 'picture-frame' ones, and new twin Windtone horns were finally loud enough to get a car-driver's attention. In mid-year, the US gas tanks adopted the beautiful 'scalloped' paintwork layout.

A linking tube between the exhausts meant that each exhaust benefitted from the extractor action in the other pipe. And because each cylinder fired alternately, each exhaust phase was absorbed by both silencers rather than just one, lowering noise levels. This meant that the UK T120s could now

ABOVE *This 1970 T120RT is actually a 750cc conversion, one of 202 done in the US to homologate for racing.*

A 'Motor Cycle Mechanics' 1969 test noted that "somehow…over the years… all the lumpiness…associated with high performance machinery has been smoothed out." The secret was that from October 1968, a crankshaft with a heavier flywheel had been fitted, and as John Nelson said: "Reduced 'the peakiness' of the engine vibration." This was done without compromising acceleration. A 1966 T120 on test with 'Cycle' had done 0 to 60mph in 5.7s. Then their 1969 model did it in five seconds flat, with its standing quarter an impressive 13.88 seconds.

'Cycle' found the 1969 handling "superb", the engine tractable and "un-cammy", though there was a distinct power band between 4,000 and 6,700 rpm (the Triumph mantra was 'Never Go More Than Seven'). With "a paint job that dares to call itself Olympic Flame and gets away with it," they judged the 1969

Bonnie, despite the arrival of the Honda-Four and the Trident, to be "one of the two or three most *desirable* motorcycles being made in the world today."

And that was about it, for the 1960s and the classic Bonnie. The peak year for US sales, 1970, brought a usefully revised engine breathing system, and a disastrous mid-year change in the gearbox to a camplate with leaf-spring, which caused a great many warranty claims right up to 1973.

However, as 'Cycle World' confirmed, the Bonnie "was still the 'in' bike with the local drive-in crowd… the most sought-after piece of merchandise by teenagers." With a version in many ways inferior on the near horizon, we'll leave the Bonneville there in 1969, when it was, as Peter Egan wrote, "the final product and distillation of everything learned about balance and proportion in the era that preceded it."

ABOVE *The good times roll. A 1968 UK T120 with Concentric carbs, a fine new front brake, double-damped front forks and an improved swinging-arm.*

RIGHT *The 1970 UK 650cc Bonneville, the last of the pure line as the storm clouds gather.*

adopt the shorter US silencers. And mid-season, the long-standing Triumph twin problem of camshaft wear was finally sorted by the surface-hardening Nitriding process.

ABOVE LEFT *A US spec 1965 Bonnie, eager-looking with swept-back exhausts and 'tear-drop' silencers.*

ABOVE *The 1966 model. The hot engine, with revised steering head angle improving handling.*

LEFT *As good as it got. A US spec 1969 T120, showing TLS front brake and Windtone horns.*

Show Me
THE MONEY

TO BE SUCCESSFUL IN THE 1960S A MANUFACTURER HAD TO CRACK THE AMERICAN MARKET.

The majority market for big British bikes in the 1960s was North America, and of that motorcycle scene Richard Renstrom wrote, with no exaggeration: "We hard-riding Yanks could wreck the best that England could produce in 10 to 15,000 miles…in drag races, hill climbs, fast road use…scrambles, turkey runs and playing in the dirt." With more money and higher octane, cheaper gasoline, young Americans could tune their engines for speed, thrash them, and then, due to weather extremes, put them away for much of the year.

Three of the band Buddy Holly and the Crickets bought British twins in the summer of 1958, two Triumphs and a 650cc Ariel. Their drummer Jerry Allison remembered "We used to ride out from Lubbock, Texas, on the Clovis road to a place called the Scout Camp, where there were a lot of hills and gullies to climb." Road bikes, playing in the dirt.

For long, often monotonous distances were involved in US highway travel. And Henry Ford's mass production meant that automobiles had been cheaper than American motorcycles, Harley Davidsons and Indians, for decades. So, motorcycles became leisure tools rather than primary transport. And the leisure meant sports riding, whether official or unofficial, as well as, increasingly, an expression of rebellion.

FIGHT FOR THE RIGHT

Post-war British export to the USA had been given a boost in Sept 1949, when the UK government devalued the pound against the dollar, which lowered the retail price of British machines nearly 20%. The light, powerful British twins and the Gold Star, Royal Enfield and Matchless singles ran rings round the heavier, mostly side-valve, home-grown products (though the latter were infinitely more durable), on or off tarmac.

BSA had established their presence in America since 1945 when Alfred Childs had arrived unsolicited at Small Heath and secured 'the agency for the 48 States'. By the 1950s this had grown to a large dealer network divided between the Rich Child Corporation of New Jersey for the Eastern States, and the

ABOVE *BSA A65-mounted 'Feets' Minnert giving it 110% against Triumph's Skip van Leuwen at the Ascot TT.*

BSAs take part, and they took the first five places.

Triumph, spearheaded by Edward Turner and Jack Sangster, had already successfully defended the British imports against a legal assault from Harley Davidson, demanding import tariffs. That story will be found in the 'Triumph in the USA' section.

The same paradoxical situation as with the home factories soon arose. BSA and Triumph dealers, and their sponsored competition riders, became fierce rivals. This rivalry soon turned bitter, especially during Edward Turner's 1957 to 1964 reign as automotive chief, when BSA dealers tended to be overlooked.

ABOVE *A BSA A65 Hornet 650, Small Heath's take on the desert sled.*

ABOVE *The BSA 1953-54 A10 Super Flash was an export-only 650cc model highly tuned for US sports riders.*

ABOVE *The pre-unit TR6 Trophy 650, the basis of many desert sleds.*

The diminutive top rider Chuck 'Feets' Minnert, so-called because of his outsize trotters, had led a BSA Gold Star 1-2-3 at the Catalina Grand Prix. He said later, "I was a BSA rider through and through. To this day I never fully trust a guy riding a Triumph." And things worsened in the mid-1960s when the amalgamation of BSA and Triumph dealers was being attempted by BSA Group management. Jack Wilson was head of Texas Triumph specialist Big D and had been behind Johnny Allen's world speed record. Of the amalgamation he said, "It's a great deal for BSA dealers, but it's like offering Triumph dealers the clap." In fact, several BSA dealers faced with the prospect, defected to the rising star of Honda and the Japanese.

EAST AND WEST
As the 1960s began and the baby boomers came of age, the US two wheel market did the opposite to the UK's: it exploded.

Hap Alzina company in San Francisco for the West.

Former Indian agent Hap, so-called because of his sunny disposition, was a major developer on US sports versions of Small Heath's machines. The ferociously fast 1953-54 plunger-framed A10 Super Flash 650, was built by BSA for export only, to Alzina's specification. It featured an alloy head; triplex primary drive chain when even the later (but slower) sporting Road Rocket model retained single chain drive; a GP carb; and an output of 42bhp, when the stock A10 only made 34. Hap would also be responsible for the later 1957-on A10 Spitfire scramblers, in many ways the forerunners of the legendary Rocket Gold Star.

An early 1950s visit from Hopwood and Perrigo led to an unsatisfactory US export spares situation being improved. With the US slogan 'Win on Sunday, Sell on Monday' now thoroughly understood by all parties, the visit also led to the development, with stronger gearboxes and valve springs, of A7 Star Twins and Gold Stars to contest the prestigious 1954 Daytona 200, half beach/half tarmac race. Alzina had to fight, nearly literally, with the AMA representatives, to let the

ABOVE Brando in 'The Wild One' as Johnny, leader of the Black Rebel Motorcycle Club, with Triumph Thunderbird.

New sales grew from 45,000 in 1960 to 298,000 in 1965, 433,000 in 1966 and 744,000 in 1967. There was a mild dip in the market due to the first major intakes of young men drafted for Vietnam. But then sales continued to rise as, returning from their year's deployment, many spent their service gratuities on the bikes they had been dreaming of.

The majority of sales during this period were due to Honda, already with 65.9% of the US market in 1963. Honda had skin in the game, since US bank loans meant that failure in the US could have broken them. Much of their success was due to the brilliant ad campaign, run in mainstream as well as specialist media, with the slogan "You Meet the Nicest People on a Honda" - cue nuns on step-through C90 Cubs.

As columnist Maynard Hershon summed up the appeal of his first bike, a 200cc Honda 1962 CB72 Hawk. "In clean-cut America…we'd never known anyone who rode a motorcycle…we certainly could not have afforded the price of admission to HD or BSA-Triumph style motorcycling. We didn't want to give up button-down shirts or khaki pants… You could own a Hawk and not have to establish a relationship with the scary guy who fixed bikes."

ABOVE The BSA A10 Spitfire scrambler, with input from Hap Alzina.

However, until 1969 at least, Edward Turner's short-term solution, that Honda introducing two-wheelers to Stateside youngsters would benefit the Group as the kids would then graduate to big British bikes, appeared to be working. It also benefitted AMC for a while, as in 1963 their importers the Berliner Corps had 7.3% of the market, or around 10,000 Norton and Matchless machines, though the figure also included Ducatis.

With both Triumph and BSA dealerships divided on an east coast and west coast basis, the east and west set-ups, particularly in the case of Triumph, were

ABOVE It's 1969, and the game changes with the movie 'Easy Rider'.

exact hour over a ten mile loop, while 'Hare scrambles' were two 50 mile loops around the same course. Entries of up to 1,000 riders meant that all but the leaders were permanently obscured in dust. Many 1960s 'desert sleds' had light-coloured seats to combat the heat effects of the relentless California sun. And Enduro-type events like the Big Bear Run would climb high into the Sierra mountains.

Triumph dealer, ISDT competitor and stuntman Bud Ekins had some tips on desert racing. At high altitudes the freezing night air could cause condensation of fuel turning to ice and messing up the carburation. He found the cure to be Wynn's oil which contained an anti-freezing agent. He also fitted smaller carburettor main jets and used the choke slide to offset the effects

at odds with each other, as well as with their rivals within the Group. The east was by some way the largest market. For competition, their forest-bound, Enduro-type events often meant that 500cc twins were the favoured tool.

Their variants became early examples of the 'street scrambler,' like the east coast Triumph T120C, which had a bash plate and high-level silencers, but still fitted a headlamp. The west coast competition bikes favoured out-and-out off-road trim for desert riding, with straight-through exhausts and no lights at all. In general, the west wanted more power, where the east sought greater reliability.

COMPETITION

US competition categories were different from European ones, and often on the wild and woolly side. The Catalina Island Grand Prix, a ten mile on and off-road loop covered ten times, was discontinued in the early 1960s due to drunken fights, with film star Lee Marvin escorted from the ferry at pistol-point. Not the Grand Prix as we knew it.

Desert race Hare 'n Hounds events usually ran in two separate 50 mile loops, but the 160 mile Barstow to Vegas race was also called Hare 'n Hounds. 'European scrambles' were run for an

ABOVE *Meriden made the most of the American Graffiti vibe to promote the 1977 T140 Bonneville.*

of altitude, gradually dropping the slide as he descended to lower levels.

On dirt track ovals, the term 'TT' was a little different from the Isle of Man's 37 mile, three-lap Tourist Trophy road race. US-style it was run on a quarter mile, kidney-shaped track on dry clay, with a jump mid-way to keep things interesting. California's premier Ascot flat track in Los Angeles included a TT course. In 1959, Daytona moved from the beach and tarmac course to the newly built, banked Daytona International Speedway, which included a 2.95-mile motorcycle circuit. Tarmac racing gained ground in America throughout the 1960s.

REBELS

The US outlaw biker scene came to prominence with a drunken weekend and a posed photo at Hollister, California. That was the basis for the

1954 Marlon Brando movie 'The Wild One,' in which Brando rode his own 1950 Triumph 650cc Thunderbird. The Triumph importers tried to stop the film in production, but in the end, while it may have damaged the reputation of motorcyclists as a group, it did the company little harm. From then on 'Rebels Rode Triumphs,' and as the 1960s unfurled there were plenty of rebels.

In fact, the real tattooed hoods, the 1% patch clubs, favoured stripped and chopped versions of the big Harley 74s for their 'Hogs'. While writing *'Hell's Angels'*, the gonzo journalist Hunter S. Thompson bought a 1965 BSA A65 Lightning Rocket 650 to ride with them, due to its superior performance and handling. In fact, the BSA, purchased new in October 1965, proved the hog riders' point, as it only spent a few months on the road. It was plagued immediately with mechanical problems. Then a couple of months later a bad 'high-side' on a wet night in Oakland, "at about 70, the top of my second gear," brought much pain plus an expensive rebuild that Thompson could only pay for by May 1966. Three months later he was badly beaten up by the Angels, and he sold the bike on and left the area.

The real Brit vs Harley match was the T120 Bonneville vs the Harley 883cc XLCH Sportster. As Tim Remus wrote, "the kid on the street wanted either a Bonnie or a Harley Sportster." The Sportster was something else, appealing to somewhere between a Triumph rebel and a full-on outlaw. It was still 100lb heavier than a T120, harder to start and didn't handle so well (but it had a magneto). Despite the Harley's extra capacity, their standing quarter speeds were only a fraction of a second different. If a Triumph twin did blow a Hog away, this was known as 'smoked ham'. *'Cycle'* called both machines "sexy and fast and with a big reputation to defend." It was a good match.

But then time moved on, with the corner turning not just because of Honda's 750-Four, but after the release of the 1969 movie *'Easy Rider'*. Fonda and Hopper rode chopped Harley customs across the American southwest and into the imaginations of millions of young riders. The chopper era had arrived, and though it would sometimes be done, the treatment didn't really suit British twins.

Norton's

TOP FEATHERBED TWINS

THE NORTON 650SS WAS CONSIDERED TOP DOG FOR SPEED, HANDLING AND ROADHOLDING.

ABOVE *The Featherbed frame was stiff without being heavy, and its handling was peerless.*

Just as the domestic motorcycle market slumped, the manufacturer which had represented the best of British produced its peak sporting roadster.

The background could not have been unhappier. In 1962 Norton was just about to lose most of its workforce and their traditional if antiquated home in Bracebridge Street, Birmingham. With it would go the famous black and silver Manx Norton ohc singles, the mainstay of British racing supremacy for four decades.

What did remain, when Norton's AMC parent pulled the plug and moved Norton production to Plumstead, southeast London, in 1963, was the Featherbed frame. It was the latter which had kept the marque more or less in contention on the tracks during the 1950s, when the engine had been faced by much more powerful continental contenders.

ROOTS

In 1962, Norton's top twin, the 650SS, appeared, after a year as the export-only 650cc Manxman in the UK. After some previous garish two-tone Norton colour schemes (the Manxman came with a red seat), the SS was offered in a plain black and silver finish. The twin engine, originally designed by Bert Hopwood in 1948-9, had now been developed by his colleague at Norton from the mid-1950s to the early 1960s, Doug Hele.

Hopwood had laid out the original 500cc twin engine in just 18 months. Having worked with Edward Turner on the evolution of the ground-breaking Triumph Speed Twin, he sought to avoid some of the latter engine's drawbacks. These originally had included a tendency to run hot. With alloy expensive and in short supply in the immediate post-war period, Hopwood's all-iron motor's cylinder head had concentrated on improved air flow. The exhaust valves were splayed and the exhaust ports wide-set and heavily finned.

Production constraints enforced a three-piece crankshaft. But the bottom end was conspicuously strong, with substantial timing-side ball journals and drive-side roller main bearings. For rigidity and oil-tightness, it featured a cylinder block with a shorter stroke of 72.6mm than the Triumph's 80mm. There were integral tunnels for the pushrods, which were operated by a single, four-lobe chain-driven camshaft set at the front of the engine. So, there was no gear-driven Triumph whirring rattle for it, or for the chain-driven, rear-mounted magneto (though the Norton's tappets did chatter). Also, there were no Triumph-type leaking separate pushrod tubes fore and aft, which had further obscured airflow. However Norton's primary chain case constructed from pressed tin could be hard to keep oil-tight.

The engine was first married to the Featherbed for 1952, and from then on that was what everyone wanted. The

ABOVE *Bert Hopwood (left) with the American ambassador and a 1961 Norton Manxman, the first, export-only, version of the 650SS.*

quick-steering frame in Wideline form gave light and precise control at speed. As alternative bike guru Royce Creasey wrote, "with the rider sitting virtually upright, their weight taken on their backside and feet, steering could be guided delicately with just the fingers."

The riding position was soon aided by the option of handlebars known as 'Norton straights'. These were said to have been adopted after a factory representative giving a talk to a club had tried to convince them that the current, swept-back bars were what customers wanted. The clubmen took him out to the parking lot and showed him that every twin there had been fitted with Vincent straights! When it came, the Norton item had a less sharp 'plumber's bend' than the Vincent's.

WINNER

For 1955, the cylinder head, always known for its exceptional breathing, had changed to alloy. A great deal of development work had been done by Hele and Hopwood on the one-off 500cc Domiracer. In 1961 this had been ridden by Tom Phillis to a sensational third place in the top Isle of Man Senior TT race, averaging 98.74mph. It had been beaten only by Mike Hailwood on a pukka Manx Norton, with an MV multi coming second. This was quite a calling card for Norton twins.

The SS head had now been reworked by Doug Hele with bigger inlet valves, and to take twin, parallel-mounted carburettors at a steep downdraught angle. The head was fitted in conjunction with a Daytona profile for the engine's

single camshaft, developed earlier for the US dual surface beach and tarmac races, with flat-based cam followers. The crankshaft had been strengthened with larger big end journals, and a heavier flywheel. This, and a stroke lengthened by 7mm from the previous Dominator 99 600cc, created the 646cc (68 x 89mm) 650SS, a tough and unfussy, tractable but very quick engine.

Riders instantly recognized this, with the 650SS voted Motor Cycle News' Machine of the Year for 1962 and 1963. In addition, Syd Lawton-prepared machines, the 'Lawton Nortons', won the leading Thruxton 500 production race for three successive years, ending in 1964. At 49bhp, the 650SS aced the contemporary Bonneville's 46bhp. UK road testers were completely impressed, with ton-plus laps of MIRA in the wet, one-way runs of 119.5mph, and road trips along the whole M1 motorway (which ended near Rugby, Warwickshire in 1964) at a steady 90mph.

The Norton's looks were equally impressive, in a British, understated way. The Featherbed frame's horizontal lines were arrow straight.

The bottom line of the tank ran into the seat base, and the horizontal grab handles; the base-line of the exhaust and silencer, which lacked the frivolity of a tail-pipe, was echoed by the three horizontal ribs on the oil tank, and the straight base of the narrow chromed tank badge and knee rubber. Combined with the aggressively steep angle of the Roadholder front forks, this was a bike which if looked at properly was as taut as an archer's shaft awaiting release. It was purposeful looking at rest, with a solid, unmistakably masculine aura compared to a Triumph twin's almost delicate air.

While the 650cc engine had reached fruition, the means to exploit it were provided by the Roadholder front forks and the Featherbed frame. On the road, the Featherbed was king. "You steer it with your nose," as one rider put it. Just looking at, or thinking of a line, got you round it, on rails.

FEATHERBED

The frame had been designed by Ulstermen Rex and Cromie McCandless. Their genius had developed Rex's ideas from swinging-arm conversions for others' frames, to a complete, all-welded chassis of their

RIGHT *A ruggedly good-looking 650SS.*

own, which they sold to Norton. All the production Featherbeds were made at specialists Reynolds Tubes. The reason was that they were Sif-bronze welded, a technique which allowed welds to be built up precisely in fillets, while Bracebridge Street only had facilities for the old hearth-brazing methods.

Frames for racers were in superior Reynolds 531 tubing, while roadster twins were in 14-gauge 'B' tubing, and arc-welded. This farming out of manufacture meant that Featherbeds could continue to be supplied after the move to Plumstead. But it did limit production numbers, at first to 70 a week, though that figure would rise, though never substantially.

The Featherbed was a duplex-loop design with a short swinging-arm. The two main loops of frame were welded to the headstock. From the headstock they angled outward and ran back horizontally as the tank top rails, with the tank resting on top of them on rubber mountings, secured down its length by a metal top strap. The twin tubes were then bent down to run behind the gearbox, and then bent forward again to pass beneath the box and engine. Bent upwards once more to form the frame's duplex front down-tubes, they were then sprung into position inside the top tube rails, where they were welded to both the rails and the headstock.

RIGHT *A 650SS, ridden hard.*

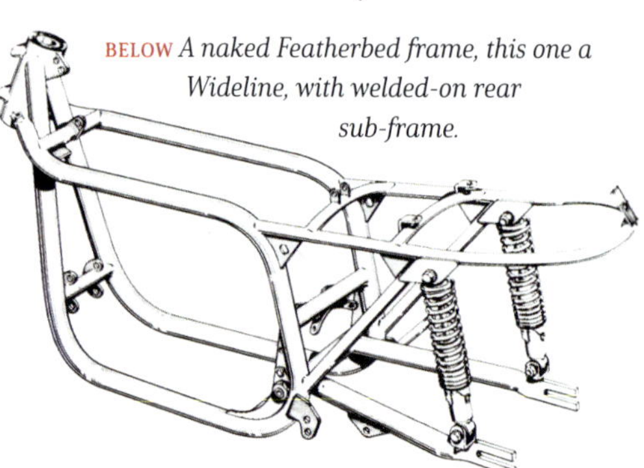

BELOW *A naked Featherbed frame, this one a Wideline, with welded-on rear sub-frame.*

This unique crossover bracing arrangement would prove exceptionally resistant to the intense torsional stresses of tarmac racing speeds. However, it would not, as we shall see, suit off-road stresses. The rear sub-frame had at first been bolted onto the main loops, but from 1955 was welded on, where Triumph's brazed frames stayed with a bolted-on sub-frame until 1971. Three of the frame's four cross-tubes, welded in to brace the main tubes, carried steel

ABOVE *A 'Wideline' Featherbed framed 500cc Dominator 88 from 1955.*

mounting plates for the engine and gearbox, one of them the head-steady. As Rex McCandless put it, "the engine was a very important part of the frame."

The 'short' Roadholder forks, so-called in comparison to early versions two inches longer, with their wide-set, substantial stanchions and alloy sliders, were also state-of-the-art. They employed genuine two-way damping. For 1964 their centres would be increased from seven to 7 3/8in, to take wider tyres for America.

The frame was changed for 1960 from the so-called 'Wideline' to the 'Slimline' version. The reason given was that at 11 ½in across, and with a broad tank and seat-nose, the Wideline could be uncomfortable for the short of stature. It could also make it hard for them to get both feet flat on the ground at rest. But the Wideline, which some argued handled a little better on track, had been lived with for eight years.

A more likely reason for the change had been so that Triumph-type rear panelling, introduced on Norton's Jubilee and Navigator unit engine light twins, could also be fitted to the larger capacity pre-unit twins. For the Slimline, the frame tubes were bent differently just above the rear gusset, kinking the back of the main loop inward, with the tubes at the front bent a little more to match. The narrower top rails permitted a slimmer seat nose and a 3.6 gallon tank, which lost the former

ABOVE *A day out in Brighton. A single carb Norton Featherbed twin with the café racer treatment.*

metal top securing strap. The new frame was entirely acceptable for the 650SS' fast road use.

ON THE ROAD

Rockers no longer had a reason to build Tritons, with one Salt Box café Triton rider describing how he could never pass his hard-riding mate's 650SS. Nortons were still pricier - £374 for a 1967 650SS compared to £355 for a Bonneville T120, but the real problem was availability. In 1963, with the move to Plumstead, less than 1,500 Norton 650s were produced. The spares situation from then on was

equally poor and 80% of Plumstead production was going to America. It was a missed opportunity, as the big Norton's quality was recognized and respected at home. In the 1960s you had to hunt hard for a second-hand 650SS.

The 650 retained reliable, self-contained magneto ignition, with a Lucas RM19 alternator for lights. Though the stock, Hele-developed engine was good enough that Syd Lawton, apart from fitting a home-brewed, Manx-derived gearbox to his production racer, stated: "We didn't tune it for extra power or performance." The only feature Lawton did not like was the crankshaft-mounted alternator. Together with the heavier clutches – the 650 Norton's got an extra plate – fitted to cope with rising power, he felt that the weight of the alternator could affect handling at racing speeds. He would partially cure this by rebuilding the wheels with the rims pulled fractionally to the left.

For daily use, starting was reliable, if you were careful not to flood the steeply angled carburettors. The engine was tractable and torquey. Handling and roadholding, wet or dry, solo or two up, was completely reliable. Stopping from the eight-inch SLS front brake was a respectable 28½ft from 30mph. The AMC separate gearbox was very good indeed. If there was a downside, it was the rather harsh ride from the Norton transmission set-up and the firm suspension necessary for

LEFT *The works 54bhp, 500cc Domiracer twin, a sensational third in the 1961 TT.*

ABOVE *The 650SS engine, with magneto and leak-prone tin primary chain case. But Nortons were more oil-tight than most.*

the fine handling, plus an unforgiving dual seat. The 650SS could be a bit of a hard taskmaster on long journeys. This, and the understated looks, may have contributed to the Norton 650 being respected rather than loved like the Bonneville.

ROCKET

But all that could be trumped by speed, which depended very much on how you rode it. Oxford student enthusiast Mike Sewell ran not a 650SS but a 600 Dominator 99, which he "tuned… with go-faster bits from the 650SS, all lightened, polished and balanced, and very carefully put together. At first, I was disappointed that after all that hard work, it would still only do 85, flat out, chin on the tank. Then I fitted a rev counter, and realized that when it was flat out, it was only doing 4,000 rpm. So, I took another fistful of throttle. The bike took off like a rocket, right up to and past 100, and I damn near fell off it. So, I fitted a quick-action throttle and rode it on the rev counter instead of the noise and vibration. From my home in Bristol to my digs in Oxford became one long racetrack…"

From 1964 the 650SS was produced alongside a 750cc version, the Norton Atlas. Before his departure to Triumph, Hele, at Berliner's request, had laid out this soft-tuned, 7.5:1 compression ratio, torquey, bored-out engine, though well aware of the vibratory results of further enlarging a parallel twin. Even so, a *'Cycle World'* test in 1965, while loving the 20mph to 109mph in top gear flexibility, called out "some very spirited shaking" at speed. Plumstead development of this engine would be part of Norton's last great leap. But before that the 650SS, discontinued in February 1968, with a single carburettor version, the 650 Mercury, for 1969, had delivered the power-with-flexibility goods. As one tester put it, "Approaches two miles a minute yet eats out of your hand."

ABOVE *Perhaps the best-looking British twin of all, in its understated way.*

BRITISH CLASSICS: MINI

Over the years there have been many classic cars, but few have the same iconic status as the Mini.

Launched in 1959 as a small, affordable family vehicle the Mini soon became a status symbol for the fashionable, an unbeatable racing machine and even a screen star. British Classics Mini takes an in-depth look at how the Mini was designed, launched, and marketed as well as the many prototype designs and model updates. There are chapters on the Cooper and variants including the Moke, estate, pickup, and van models, plus a section on the BMW MINI. Lavishly illustrated, this is a publication no Mini enthusiast will want to miss.

116pp

Author: *Mike Renaut*

ONLY £8.99 PLUS FREE P&P*

*Free 2nd class P&P on all UK & BFPO orders. Overseas charges apply.

ORDER DIRECT

ALSO AVAILABLE FROM **WHSmith** AND ALL LEADING NEWSAGENTS

SUBSCRIBERS CALL FOR YOUR £2 DISCOUNT!

Free P&P* when you order online at
shop.keypublishing.com/ClassicMini

OR

Call UK: **01780 480404**
Overseas: **+44 1780 480404**

IF YOU ARE INTERESTED IN **BRITISH CLASSICS: MINI**, YOU MAY ALSO LIKE...

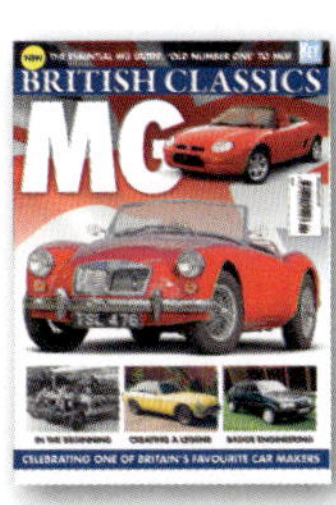
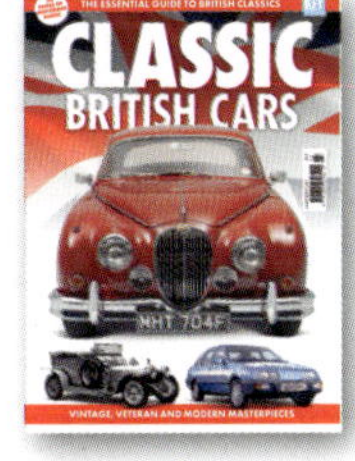

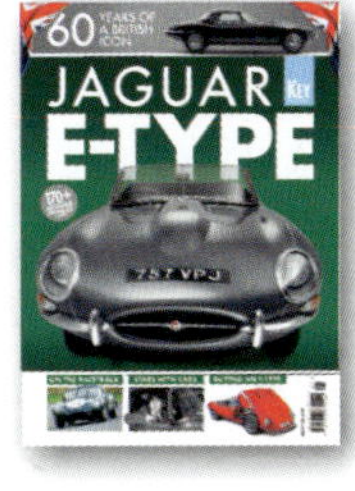

BSA and Triumph
UNIT SINGLES

SINGLE CYLINDER UNIT 'THUMPERS' WERE A POPULAR OFFERING FROM BIRMINGHAM. SMALL HEATH MANUFACTURED BOTH VERSIONS OF THESE OFTEN FLAWED ONE-POT WONDERS.

ABOVE LEFT *BSA C15 Star making everyone happy, in 1960 Almond Green optional colour scheme.*

ABOVE *Old-style BSA production line in 1960, producing the popular C15.*

It started with the C15 Star. Announced late in 1958 and derived from Edward Turner's 200cc Tiger Cub, the 247cc (67 x 70mm) 'Ceefer' engine featured an upright cylinder. The BSA-type styling was attractive, with clean lines and a cheerful chromed tank plus either red or blue paintwork. It looked like a proper, full-size motorcycle, yet only weighed 280lb dry.

Unfortunately, the engine design also came with the Tiger Cub's problems fully intact. BSA design office apprentice Ed Wright summed these up as "poor distributor drive, weak main bearings, and a flimsy gearbox." He was not alone in wondering about "the strange lack of feedback from Triumph on the problems they must have experienced with the Tiger Cub." For instance, the wear-prone clamp holding the car-type distributor, which protruded from the top right side of the crankcase, was the exact same item as on the Cub.

However, young Wright had also felt that "the C15, though under-engineered, was a breath of fresh air." It was aimed at the emerging younger market, who wanted something light, attractive, uncluttered and modern looking. On 17in wheels with a low seat height, female riders were not excluded.

The problem was that the new 250 had been a rush job. New Automotive Division chief Edward Turner had insisted it be ready for the 1959 model year. The result, in the words of BSA veteran Norman Vanhouse, was that "the normal development was completely dispensed with, no prototype was built, completed drawings were passed straight to the production team, so that the first example of the new design to be started up was a production model." Journalist Bob Currie had that dubious pleasure, and promptly broke the kickstart ratchet.

MAKING SOMETHING OF IT

Vanhouse continued, "When the machines came off the track, the situation was chaotic, with all members of the experimental department pressed into service on rectification work." The initial problem was discovered to be that the kickstart pawls had gone through with their edges overhardened, and were thus too brittle.

New ones were fitted, but the kickstart mechanism design itself, which drove the layshaft bottom gear with a pawl and an internal ratchet, was the problem. It also put the kickstart pedal and the right-side footrest uncomfortably close together. The design problem was not dealt with until 1965. Before that, many owners regularly had to push-start their C15s when the mechanism failed.

Turner had left BSA's head of design, Bert Perrigo, to sort out this and many other problems. "In the end," said Perrigo, "we made something of it." In this BSA were assisted by two factors. The 1961 250cc learner limit helped ensure that the model was a sales success, with 46,000 250s sold from 1959 to 1965.

Secondly, this was the era when lightweight two-strokes in trials and scrambles were ousting big heavyweight bangers like the Gold Star. BSA were winners off-road, and their Comp shop seized on the new unit motors, developing out their faults and exploiting their light weight. Works ace John Banks said of the later 500cc scramblers: "The two-strokes were quick, but they had no bottom end. The BSA was as fast and it was so good out of the corners." Jeff Smith on the Victor scrambler would win the motocross World Championship in 1964 and 1965.

THE C15 GOES FORTH

That was a long way from the early 7.25:1 compression ratio C15, which produced 15bhp @ 7,000 rpm and was capable of a top speed of barely 70mph. The unit engine sat in a single front downtube cradle frame and was mounted noticeably off-centre. Electrics were via an alternator, with all the fragility and overcharging problems this then involved, and thin joint faces meant inevitable oil leaks. Six-inch diameter full-width hub brakes both front and rear were not a strong suit either.

The distributor being prone to slipping when its clamp was worn could alter the timing. That was serious, as both

ABOVE *The clean-living C15 image. But how long will that skirt stay spotless?*

the plain big end with its shell bearings, and the main bearings, particularly the timing-side bush, could fail if the timing became over-advanced. The gearbox suffered from the limited space available with unit construction. And finally, the engine could be damaged if you rode it like a traditional single, plonking along at low revs in a high gear – you needed to use the gears.

Still, a mid-1960s' Rider's Report in Motor Cycle on the C15 was largely positive. If they didn't go wrong right away, and they bedded in, C15s were judged reliable enough. The good riding position, standard of finish, the acceleration in second and third gears, fuel economy of up to 90mpg, and a 50 – 55mph cruising speed, were all

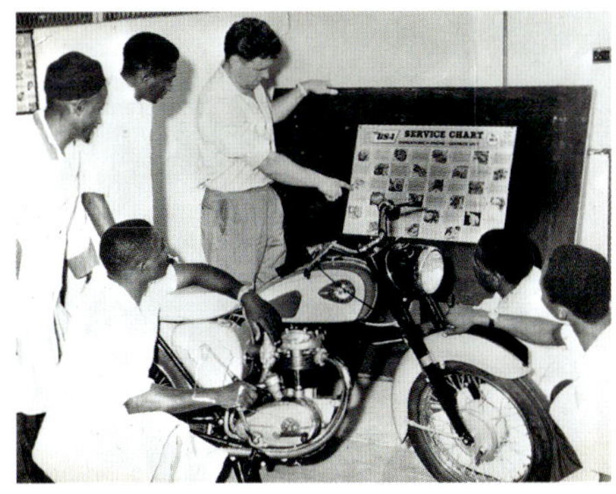

ABOVE *In former Tanganyika, a service school for the C15.*

appreciated. The skimpy ½in x 5/8in rear chain could need replacing after 2,000 miles, but for a first bike, you could do worse.

BETTER

And gradually, things improved. The competition variants came in from the start, and 1961 brought the 350cc B40 version, bored out to 79mm. It was a commercial failure, with just 8,000 sold until it was dropped in 1966, but it would have a second life, and many now judge it the best all-rounder of the unit engines. Launches for 1961 also saw the SS80 sports C15, tuned with higher compression, a hotter camshaft, and importantly, a stronger double caged roller bearing big end. The C15

BELOW *A 1965 B40 Star 350, still with distributor electrics as it was to be discontinued.*

BELOW *A C15-engined off-roader with modern tweaks.*

adopted this for 1964, along with an 8.0:1 compression ratio – learner riders wanted the status of a performance machine, even if it wasn't suitable.

The following year, 1965 was a 'big change' year for the unit singles, the newer model saw the distributor replaced by points mounted in the timing chest. The gearbox adopted the stronger, competition-bred stub-tooth form, and the kickstart mechanism changed to a tougher face ratchet mounted on the end of the mainshaft and turned by a quadrant.

For 1966, the SS80 changed its name to the C15 Sportsman, which with all the previous years' improvements, was reckoned by many to be the best 250cc variant. An over-the-counter

version of the 441cc Victor GP scrambler was offered, with 11.5:1 compression, an oil-bearing frame in Reynolds 531, and a damped fork developed by Jeff Smith. With it there came the 441cc B44VE Victor Enduro, a trail bike with a detuned engine that used a linered barrel.

Meanwhile the abandoned 350cc B40 was revived by a Ministry of Defence order for 2,000 of them. The B40WD used the C15T frame, dropped the compression, fitted a quickly

detachable rear wheel, a detachable oil filter, 12-volt electrics, and a fully enclosed rear chainguard. The only downside was a small carburettor with a butterfly throttle. Entering service in 1967, 3,079 were produced. There was also a large order from the Australian forces, and then for a further 1,000 semi-civilianised versions, sold as the Rough Rider.

HERE WE GO

In July 1966, all the 250s were fitted with the Victor's bottom end featuring ball and roller main bearings, a stronger crankcase, revised lubrication with an end-fed crankshaft, and a bigger version of the model's two-fixing alloy oil pump, though this would remain unsatisfactorily prone to distortion.

These C15s only had a brief life, as for 1967 i.e. from Sept 1966 when the new model year began, the new 24bhp C25 Barracuda was launched. It was aimed squarely at the US market, where the same model appeared as the B25 Starfire.

It was 35lb heavier than the original C15 at 315lb, and the C25 featured a new square-finned alloy barrel, on the Victor crankcase. Within it, a new one-piece forged crankshaft ran on ball and roller mains, but the light alloy con rod still featured a split big end with shell bearings. Compression ratio was a stonking 9.5:1. The drive chain size increased to 5/8in x ¼ in. The C25 was flamboyantly styled, with a 'Bushfire

ABOVE *BSA's World Champion scrambler Jeff Smith gets airborne on a works unit single.*

ABOVE *Hard man Jeff Smith with a works BSA Victor scrambler.*

ABOVE RIGHT *A 1967 WDB40 on show. New life for the 350.*

ABOVE *Unit singles (Right) coming off BSA's semi-automated production line in 1965.*

ABOVE *A 1967 US export B44VE Victor Enduro. Note the round barrel and long forks.*

ABOVE *The second coming. A US B25 Starfire 250 for 1968.*

Orange' and white colour scheme for its sculpted fibreglass 1¾ gallon fuel tank and side-panels, and a separate chromed headlamp. Top speed was 90mph. It was joined by the B44VR Victor Roadster, similarly styled, and with a similar top speed.

Amal Concentric carburettors were introduced, the C25's initially with a massive 220 main jet, reduced the following year to 170. Brakes became seven-inch all round. In the 250cc engine, the inlet valve was enlarged, and a fiercely profiled cam was fitted. That, and the shell big end bearings, contributed to the C25/B25 engine's grenade-like reputation.

Henry Vale at Triumph later pinpointed how basic engineering and practicality had been ignored in pursuit of power. "The B25's cam was too fierce for the tappets, and used to break tappet feet. It also kicked back viciously if the starting drill was messed up." The absence of a

choke on the B25's Concentric carb didn't help cold starting. This was no longer a suitable machine for learners.

For 1968 the UK Barracuda became the Starfire, and along with the rest of the range was US-export styled, with high bars, gaitered forks, and reflectors – a legal requirement in the US. The 441cc Victor Roadster became the B44 Shooting Star. With a less frenetic 5,750 rpm at maximum power, it did everything the B25 Starfire did, only in a more relaxed and flexible fashion. For to exploit its performance, the 250 had to rev towards its 8,250rpm max through the gears. Both machines' short (52in) wheelbase and high ground clearance meant that though they handled well on all surfaces and accelerated exhilaratingly, the front end could be on the light side. The frame, derived from the C15 competition models, was in Norman Vanhouse's view: "Superb."

ENTER THE TWUD

For 1968, the group launched a Triumph-badged version of the 250, the TR25W. Re-styled, with a different tank, these Triumphs were built at BSA, and detuned to 22bhp. US dealers disgustedly referred to them as 'the Twud.' Severe unreliability

was held to be a combination of poor Small Heath build quality and possible sabotage. In the UK Triumph weren't too keen either. "With all its aftermarket problems," said Meriden tester Jim Lee, "the service department hated 'em."

In 1969 the 441cc models were split. There was the previous Victor Enduro, now the Victor Special, with round barrel and the older forks, and export only. The 250cc Starfire could also be bought, for export only, in trail form, with a high-level exhaust on the left, wide bars and a small tank part-painted yellow to offer some protection from deer hunters! The B44 Shooting Star, and the 250 Starfire, now fitted Triumph's genuinely two-way damped fork internals. These were in a new, slightly shorter front fork, which noticeably improved the problem of the light front end.

They also adopted seven-inch versions of Triumph's excellent TLS front brake. For 1969 also, joint faces in the crankcase and primary chain case were widened 15% to counter oil leaks. A steel 3 ¼ -gallon petrol tank and side-panels supplanted the fibreglass, for both capacities in a more sober blue colour.

Aside from a finally satisfactory three-point fixing, iron oil pump for 1970, that was it for the unit singles, bar the last dramatic 1971-72 oil-in-frame incarnations. Sometimes likeable but rarely quite reliable, the range lacked the dependability of their pre-unit forebears. They were the opposite of relaxed, they were busy, even frenetic. As Jeff Smith put it: "The later (unit) BSAs I rode felt like they were working hard to make their power."

AMC
TWINS

BIGGER WAS NOT ALWAYS BETTER.

ABOVE *AMC's excellent 500cc twin in Matchless G9 Super Clubman form, with 'Jampot' rear suspension units.*

AJS/Matchless 650 twins had a brief moment of glory in the early 1960s. Trailing tales of broken cranks and bad vibration, the AJS Model 31/Matchless G12, especially in CSR form, came good for two or three years as exhilarating accelerators with a 'ripping calico' exhaust note.

The AMC twin had started out different and remained that way. Designer Phil Walker's 1949 engine layout featured separate cylinders beneath a common cylinder head in alloy. But the most remarkable feature was the crankshaft's third, middle main bearing. Coupled with being the only UK marque other than Royal Enfield offering swinging-arm rear suspension on their production machines, this brought the new twin a lot of attention.

The third bearing was intended to stop the crankshaft acting as a skipping rope between the bearings at each end. The middle bearing, with split shells like a big end, decreased wear on the other two mains. Also, by keeping the pistons reasonably parallel and central in the bore, it slowed barrel wear appreciably, and contributed to the AMC 500 twin engine's well-known longevity.

THE MIDDLE MAIN

The configuration did slow the engine slightly and make it a little less free revving than the Triumph opposition. And detractors would say that the way it prevented the crankshaft flexing might have increased vibration for the rider, rather than the opposite. In addition, the middle main was sandwiched between twin, full disc flywheels. The bearing was carried on a detachable location web, and not very rigidly located by the web's six puny ¼in anchor studs. Possibly it was not securely enough located to prevent vibration.

That was no problem for the first, softer, 500cc twins. The 500s were put together with exceptional care. Their flywheels were balanced, and pairs of con rods made and marked together, then weighed to within 10 grams of each other, as were the pistons. "They were a marvellous engine," recalled comp shop chief Wally Wyatt. "I stripped a German rider's bike with 83,000 miles up – it didn't need a thing." They were also strong, and quick enough, at over 90mph in export 'Sport Twin' mode. Works riders on 500cc twins took ISDT Gold from 1951 to 1953. In 1952 America, Bud Ekins, before he moved

to Triumphs, won the Big Bear Run on a Matchless G9. But a G45 full racing twin proved unsuccessful.

The 500cc twin category, however, as with all the other marques bar Triumph's T100 Daytona, fell out of favour as the 1950s closed. There had also been a 600cc twin, the G11/Model 30, from 1956 to 1958, notably quick in 1958-only CSR

ABOVE *A Matchless 650cc engine with a 1960-on cylinder head and AMC gearbox. The timing cover differed from that found on AJS machines.*

form, but a harsher ride. The last 500cc twins would be made in 1961. In both the British cafes, and the competition-oriented American market that was opening up courtesy of new importer Joe Berliner, 650s were the thing.

INTO THE 1960S

There were some problems for AMC with the 650cc capacity. The 600cc, bored out to 79mm, had revealed that the separate cylinders with their centre lines a set distance apart, imposed a limit on cylinder boring. Later, when an AMC 750cc was attempted in 1962, only a couple of hundred were produced before it became clear that there was insufficient metal at the cylinder joints. So, the only way was up, with a long throw crankshaft giving 72 x 79.3 mm, 646cc capacity. After production for export-only in 1958, the 650cc was released in the UK for 1959, the peak year for new sales, when the T120 Bonneville was launched.

There were immediate troubles with AMC's 650, but even after these were mostly sorted out, there was an underlying missed opportunity. As Plumstead road tester Harry Winch later put it, this was down to: "Management's inability to listen. From 1958 to 1962 was the true age of the coffee bar cowboy, with the Bonneville and BSA's Super Rocket all selling well. That was when the CSR was needed – that basic look was nice. And it had already been about, from the early Fifties – in the shape of our ISDT twins. Instruments on brackets, siamesed exhausts, upswept pipes, it was basically the look of the CSR." But though an export-oriented, street scrambler CSR version of the 650 was available in the UK in limited numbers from 1959, "they didn't come out with the first (twin-carb) race kit until 1962," Harry continued. "Too late. It was very short-sighted."

Before then there was trouble. Primarily, when the 650 was ridden hard, crankshafts broke. Despite the AMC ban on road tests until 1961, word

ABOVE *A 1960 AJS 500cc Model 20 CSR. Blue was AJS' signature colour, red was for Matchless.*

of this spread. Initially some thought that, because the standard 650 was equipped with a crankshaft-mounted alternator on the drive side, where the fractures occurred, the added torsional stresses from the alternator's weight might be the cause.

The AMC engineers consulted their friends at Dagenham Ford, for whom Plumstead undertook contract work. The accepted narrative since then has been that the latter advised a change to nodular iron for the crankshaft, and

that this was successfully introduced for 1961. The truth was more nuanced. The crankshafts were always made of Meehanite® nodular iron. The new specification was for SGI, spheroidal graphite iron, and there were problems with the early versions of these.

The Ford metallurgists, who used SGI for the crankshafts of their Anglia cars, knew that with SGI a crank had to be ground in the direction of travel, for its microscopic particles to 'lay' one way, like a cat's fur. Otherwise stress points and fractures would ensue. After that procedure was adopted by AMC, the breakages ceased. There was no sharply

ABOVE *The 650cc Matchless CSR, a beefy sports roadster.*

ABOVE *A 1963 Matchless Monarch G12 CSR 650. The original siamesed exhaust has been replaced.*

handling improved perceptibly. It was heavier, and quite tall with a 31in seat height. Its higher centre of gravity required some conscious effort steering, but it could be heeled over hard, held the road well and steered excellently. There was vestigial rear end weaving on bumpy bends at 70mph, but this was never alarming or dangerous. The experienced Main-Smith considered it second only to the Featherbed.

The CSR now had a little more power than the contemporary Bonneville. But Williams had gone for a spread of power rather than straight top speed. The 650cc CSR was good for 104 or 105mph, with one on test with 'Motor Cycle' topping 108mph at MIRA in 1961. It was conspicuously light for a 650, at 380lb. But more importantly, the free breathing 650 had been transformed into a zestful accelerator

defined change to the new cranks. It began during 1960, with the cranks being bought-in in batches of 20 to 40, and supplied at first in machines for police riders, production racers and favoured clients. By the 1962 season, nothing but the new cranks were being used.

The other main AJS/Matchless 650 problem was vibration, and not just at high speed. Journalist Bruce Main-Smith's 1959 G12 CSR split 15 petrol tanks in 32,000 miles. It wasn't good news for the new 4¼ gallon, seam-on-the-top-centre-line tank! Another scribe, Vic Willoughby, split his standard G12's tank also. But these gentlemen regularly cruised at 90mph. Main-Smith also felt that the Teledraulic forks were showing their age and chattering at speed, until he modified them. But he found the 650 comfortable, including two-up, a good starter with a lovely exhaust note and excellent handling. And he said that it shook less than his next bike, a 650cc Triumph SAINT!

LEAPS AND BOUNDS

Meanwhile, 1960 brought two major advances. Plumstead's top designer Jack Williams had redesigned the twin's cylinder head. He laid out the new head, still alloy, with additional cooling fins, including three transverse fins under each exhaust port. The top spigot of the barrel was thickened and a recess cast in the head to take it. Holding-down bolts were enlarged.

ABOVE *The 1958-only, 100mph 600cc Matchless G11 CSR. The siamesed exhaust gave an extra 2.5bhp.*

Internally the combustion chambers became hemispherical and the pistons flat top. The inlet tracts were made curved to impart swirl to the incoming mixture, and the valves given reduced angles. Valve timing was changed, and two-rate valve springs employed, along with a new inlet camshaft. AMC were not releasing output figures, but Williams told Main-Smith that in CSR form, the engine produced 47.5bhp.

The other piece of progress had been the 1960 adoption of a new duplex downtube frame, still hearth-brazed, but better able to handle the 650's performance. With three-point tank mounting, and a slightly steeper steering head angle than the single downtube frame it replaced, the already good

up to 90mph, while still maintaining good town manners. That was aided by manual advance/retard control for the magneto, which the CSR still retained, along with a dynamo. The latter would be replaced by an alternator for 1962.

The performance point was effectively made when the Isle of Man TT marshals chose the model for their duties in 1961. That was after 1960's seven-hour Thruxton 500 production race victory by an AJS Model 31 CSR, three laps ahead of the nearest Triumph.

LOOKING GOOD, GOING WELL

What CSR stood for is arguable. Main-Smith was told 'Competition Springer Racing' but pointed out that Plumstead

ABOVE *The AJS Hurricane version of the 650cc CSR twin. The two bulges on the timing cover housed the engine's twin oil pumps.*

hadn't produced an unsprung machine for over a decade. 'Competition Sports Roadster'? Maybe, but the café crowd knew it was for 'Coffee Shop Racer'.

The CSR specification included 8.5:1 compression ratio, slightly forward-slanted rear Girling units, with until 1963, unique clevis (stirrup-shaped) lower mountings, siamesed exhaust system, and the scrambler frame. There were the skimpy alloy mudguards that the lads loved, a cut-down (uncomfortable) seat and an open-sided rear light mounting. There were no twinned instruments as standard, but from 1960 a rev counter was an optional extra and could be mounted on a separate chromed plate.

Mounting twin carburettors on the separate cylinders had always been problematic, but from 1962 a speed kit was offered, with twin Monoblocs and manifold, 10:1 compression pistons and a special camshaft, giving 110mph-plus but sacrificing the tractability. And as Harry Winch said: "The secret with CSRs seemed to be putting them together properly."

Their faults included rapid camshaft wear, clutch slip, oil leaks at the base of the cylinder and lingering vibration. The seven-inch brakes were never more than adequate. They cost 10% more than a Bonneville and were scarcer, with AMC production low and much of it going to Joe Berliner in New Jersey. It was Berliner who asked for 1962's flamboyant 'knee-knocker' metal tank badges, which added bling but chafed riders' knees. The following year these went on a redesigned tank with more comfortable knee recesses. Meanwhile the range had been given names which everyone ignored, though the Model 31 CSR's 'Hurricane' was a good one. It would turn up again 10 years later on a factory custom Triumph triple.

As former-rocker and hybrid specialist Paul Morin put it: "In the early days (around 1962) the CSR 650s were respected, but not in the later (1964-on) period – they were then too slow in comparison with the Bonnie." But with AMC's finances in free fall, the pure Plumstead twin line was coming to an end. In mid-1963, 'cigar' silencers from Norton, now moved into Plumstead, were introduced. For 1964, Norton Roadholder forks, eight-inch SLS front brake and oil pump went on the AMC 650s, arguably improvements but definitely dilutions. "Matchless had been a well-built machine," observed design engineer Tony Denniss. Of the CSR design, works racer Alan Shepherd called Jack Williams "a top-line engineer who wasn't really given a chance. They were always short of money and Jack performed miracles on a shoe-string budget."

LEFT *The final stage. A 1965 AJS Model 33 CSR 750, with Norton silencers, Atlas engine and Roadholder front end*

Triumph
IN AMERICA

FOR YOUNG AMERICANS, BIKES MEANT COMPETITION. FOR MANUFACTURERS, AMERICA MEANT OPPORTUNITY.

Edward Turner had established a foothold for Triumph in the USA before World War Two. In California in the summer of 1939, he became friends with Bill Johnson, a well-to-do lawyer who owned an Ariel Square Four. Johnson also ran British American Motors in Los Angeles.

Turner persuaded him to expand the business to become Johnson's Motors Inc (JoMo), marketing Ariel and Indian motorcycles. The new Triumph Speed Twins arrived, and by 1940 were a runaway success on the racetracks. In late 1944, Johnson secured the direct sales rights for Triumphs in Southern California.

Immediately post-war, Turner persuaded his friend Johnson, who had moved to glass-walled premises in Pasadena, to re-model the place along the lines of a Cadillac dealership, with a spotless interior and neon signage. He gave Johnson Triumph distribution rights for the whole USA. Johnson built up a team which included Pete Colman, a former international speedway and flat-track racer, a top tuner, and later a very influential BSA/Triumph executive.

TRICOR

By 1950, with BSA's American network growing, California-based Johnson was selling 1,000 Triumphs a year, but Turner could see that this was far below the vast nation's potential. Johnson employed just two 'road men' to cover dealerships across the whole country. Turner took advice from a market research outfit, and then he and Sangster appointed Coventry-born expatriate Denis McCormack to run the Triumph Corporation (TriCor) based in north Baltimore on the eastern coast. TriCor was a wholly owned Meriden subsidiary from the start. Turner remained on good terms with Johnson, who kept his operation, now covering the 19 Western states, and was made a vice-president of TriCor.

When Harley-Davidson prohibited their own dealers from handling British imports, McCormack recruited dealers from the failing Indian company, from returning servicemen using their gratuities to start a business, and even from some JoMo dealers. That began the bitterness between the majority market east, and the west.

Harley-Davidson used the AMA to limit the ohv Brits to 500cc in most Class C events, against the side-valve 750cc Harleys. For unlimited US TT racing, they allowed 650cc imports, but against 1,200cc Harleys, though Triumphs still won anyway. Then, struggling with motorcycles that were not only 200lb lighter but 20% cheaper after the 1949 devaluation of the pound, Harley went to court.

RIGHT *The 1965 T120 TT Special. 'It was a rocket!'*

ABOVE *A 750cc flat tracker in Trackmaster frame.*

LEFT *The legendary Gary Nixon on a C.R. Axell-tuned special flat-track racer.*

ABOVE *Gene Romero on flat-track Triumph 500 at Ascot in 1967, with a BSA pressing hard.*

They demanded that the existing 10% import tariff on the British bikes be raised to 40%. McCormack's expensive legal team argued, successfully, that the importers' fast middleweights filled a market sector which the home team were ignoring. By the mid-1950s, sales and race success had bred a strong and loyal dealer network.

In 1950, TriCor's service manager Rod Coates had won the 100-mile amateur race at Daytona on an alloy-engined Triumph 500 Grand Prix. Coates now set up training schools for Triumph dealers, sometimes visited by Turner himself. They successfully taught not just servicing, but stocking, financing, and promotion. This well-organized set-up gave the edge to Triumph when the 1960s boom years arrived.

There was also the feedback to Meriden, via visits from US executives and dealers, as well as the below-the-counter introduction of US performance parts to the Meriden Comp shop, which contributed to the evolution of the Bonneville. BSA by contrast, wrote Hopwood, "suffered a significant lack of communication with the US dealer organization, which meant that we worked in a partial vacuum at Small Heath."

IN THE DIRT

The Americans considered any imported motorcycle a racer. While Triumph's weaknesses might be revealed in tarmac racing, as demonstrated by BSA Gold Star domination of the Isle of Man Clubman's TT, it was different on the dirt. This was the USA's home-grown competition setting. In the mid-west and rural California, dirt-track motorcycle racing at county fairgrounds, on mile-long horse-racing ovals or shorter tracks, became an established, semi-respected feature, and led to dedicated oval arenas also used by race cars.

Unlike speedway's shale, dirt was unpredictable, varying with local geology and weather. There were mid-west 'cushion' tracks with crumbly dirt, and 'groove' tracks with hard, slick, oil-and-rubber paths; and many variations of the two. Los Angeles' Ascot was groove track by day, cushion by night.

With no brakes, the rider went into turns still under acceleration, then threw the wheels out of alignment so that the back one, in its struggles to line up again, would run counter to the dirt and slow the bike. The rider had to keep the wheels that way just long enough to be able to have them back in a straight line when the time came to power on again out of the corner. The riders wore iron skid soles on their left boots, to flirt with the surface on the turns.

There was the noise on open pipes, the rooster tails of dirt half the height of the stadium when clutches dropped at the start, and the sight of a line of bikes 'drafting' in each other's slip-streams, ready to catapult out and ahead on the turn. These things made flat-track racing a memorable spectacle, with the added element of the aviating jump in US TT courses – Ascot had both types.

The same power characteristics that made the 500cc and 650cc Triumphs good on the dirt-tracks also made them excel in desert racing. There the tool of choice was the 650cc TR6 Trophy, sometimes referred to less than accurately as 'a single-carb Bonnie.' These desert sleds were based first on the pre-unit TR6/B Trophy Bird, and then the TR6C, often also the favourite twin among Meriden testers.

"We ruled the desert," said Pete Colman, and the high-pipe Trophies, with re-wired electrics, proper air filters, and sometimes kicked-out front ends, did dominate the mass races for many years, until the competitions were stopped during the 1970s. By 1966, in fact, Triumph had won more cross-country events, US scrambles and US TT races than all the other makes put together. They had also re-taken the world land speed record in 1962.

THE BIG TIME

Triumph did not, however, often succeed at the highest level of US motorcycle sport. From 1954, the points-based AMA Grand National Championships began, a mixture of mile and half mile flat-track events, and partial-tarmac events like Daytona and Catalina – the top riders had to be versatile.

For the following 10 years, Triumph won just 15 of the 139 National events. BSA did a little better, with 24 thanks to the Gold Star. But the Championships were dominated by the big Harley-Davidson side-valve twins. The reason was not just the AMA-imposed capacity restrictions on the ohv imports. Harley spent heavily, on engineering development and on top riders like 'Black' Bart Markel. Neither Meriden, under the race-averse Edward Turner until 1964, nor TriCor or JoMo, would or could commit that much money.

ABOVE *America incarnate, a 1965 TT Special 650. And they rode it on the road!*

BELOW LEFT *Gene Romero on a Trackmaster-framed 750cc Triumph in 1970, his championship year.*

This changed under Harry Sturgeon. TriCor had already been building rapid racers based on the 500cc unit T100, and one had even won at Daytona in 1962. When Sturgeon sent Doug Hele, with six machines put together by Meriden Experimental, to contest Daytona for 1966, he faced covert opposition from both TriCor and JoMo. At the latter, after Bill Johnson's death in 1962, Pete Colman had become more influential. In 1966's attempted amalgamation of Triumph and BSA dealers, Colman had helped reconcile Triumph men to the unpopular move.

Colman foresaw an eventual wholly owned BSA and Triumph subsidiary in the US. This would come about late in 1968, after Hap Alzina sold the group West Coast BSA, when he retired. To build up power and influence, Colman sided with BSA group management against Meriden's efforts, including the triples which he contributed to delaying.

At Daytona that year, at first this seemed justified, as Hele's T100s were faster but far less reliable than the US versions. One problem area with Hele's engines was their aluminium tappet blocks distorting. Yet with just one engine surviving, Hele had coolly contacted the UK factory, and had a batch of cast iron tappet blocks made up and flown over just in time. In the race, Texan Buddy Elmore rode the sole Hele-engined machine to victory. Doug did acknowledge

new, more powerful version of their KR side-valve. This was the year that AMA rules changed to allow ohv 750s in flat-track, and from 1970, in road racing. The 750cc BSA/Triumph triples arrived. But the heavier triples proved unsuitable on the dirt. TriCor's Rod Coates arranged for a 750cc twin to be put together in America for 1970, using one of the several existing conversion kits, this one from Sonny Routt, with cast iron barrels giving a 79mm bore. To satisfy homologation requirements 204 of them were built, but they still had to be passed off as 650s to AMA inspectors, as they hadn't been built at Meriden.

Earlier, both Van Leuwen and Eddie Mulder from 1963 had ridden 650s produced by Meriden to JoMo's specifications. They were dubbed 'TT Specials' after their immediate race success. Mulder said: "The TT Special was an excellent TT bike right out of the box, with one of the best chassis of any stock motorcycle. It was a rocket."

With 11.2:1 compression ratio, hot cams, ET (Energy Transfer) ignition (which Pete Colman had managed to get to work efficiently), and open exhausts tucked under the crankcase, it was a 54bhp, 120mph missile. Yet as 'Cycle World' noted, "many people are buying this for

ABOVE *A 1968 US spec T120 Bonneville. 'The more you ride it, the more you like it.'*

ABOVE *The 1967 season was the final year for the iconic T120 TT Special.*

the value of US input, like TriCor's eutectic hardening process for the wear-prone camshafts. But it was Meriden's Experimental team who had carried the day.

The following year brought not only a Triumph 1-2-3 at Daytona, but this also formed part of their first victory in the AMA National Championships, for TriCor's top rider, red-headed Gary Nixon. And Nixon did it again for 1968. At the end of that year, newcomer Peter Thornton was chosen, over TriCor's experienced Denis McCormack, to head the new amalgamated BSA Inc which included Triumph, with a total of 1,600 sales outlets, against Honda's 2,000.

Thornton chose to site the new organization's HQ in Duarte, California, another blow to the east. McCormack was left a bitter man. It seems Thornton was under instructions from the BSA Group, with its pro-BSA CEO Lionel Jofeh, to favour the BSA marque, and to spend whatever it took to make them win. Thornton's race expenditure for the 1970-71 season was said to be $1 million.

The 1969 season saw Harley fighting back to win the championships with a

Gene 'Burrito' Romero rode a 71bhp version, tuned by California's C.R.Axtell, to victory in 1970's AMA Championship, where BSA/Triumph took the first five places. At Daytona it was the triples' turn. The UK bikes from Meriden Experimental were there alongside a US contingent under Pete Colman. The latter confronted Hele on the night before the race, claiming he had twins that would leave the triples for dead (after Romero's Trident had qualified at over 164mph), and that he would shop Hele's triples for their barely homologated five-speed gearboxes! Hele ignored him. The great Dick Mann's Honda CR750 won, but Romero and Don Castro's triples were second and third.

ZOOM!

One area where the 750cc twins excelled were the US TT races, with their jump. Triumph's star ride was Skip Van Leuwen ('Van Loony'), who won four TT Nationals between 1967 and 1969. The latter year saw the introduction of the popular Trackmaster oil-bearing, twin downtube frame of nickel-plated 4130 tubing, which Van Leuwen successfully used with the 750cc engine.

ordinary street riding – and it is mild enough for that sort of riding too." If you wore ear plugs! A classic case of Triumph twin versatility, even in a machine that exemplified the west coast's pursuit of power at all costs.

The TT Special indicated the typical young 1960s Triumph rider, rebelliously disdainful of anti-social elements like noise, up to a point. They rode machines with styling "a bit on the garish side, but in a pleasant way," as 'Cycle Guide' observed. The 1968 Bonneville thought 'Cycle World', was "an understated stud machine…if you are a sporting rider and deem yourself a bit of a jockey… Performance-plus…Flashiness in a moderate way, and respectable handling. Like the Harley Sportster, the Bonneville is a stud bike, although the two images aren't quite the same."

Before 1970, Triumph's top US sales year, 'Cycle Guide' on a T120, simply summed up the heart of the Triumph twins' appeal. "The bike has a great deal of personality… The more you ride it, the more you like it…For sheer feel it's very difficult to find anything better than the Bonnie. This feel is what endears itself to the owner."

BSA TWINS

SOLID BIRMINGHAM TWINS WITH 'THE WATER-MELON ENGINE'.

BSA's 500cc A50 and 650cc A65 were always the low men on the 1960s twins' totem pole. Triumph's Bonneville ruled, the Norton 650 was respected, but the unit BSAs – not so much.

Rockers had favoured the sports pre-unit BSA twins, the A10 Road Rocket and Super Rocket, but as café racer Mike Clay observed, "to the café crowd (the unit A65s) were hideous…a big bike engine needs to look knobbly."

the timing side, the same plain bush was fitted as before, though increased in size. This was to be the engine's Achilles heel, as with wear or when ridden really hard, the bush could turn and cut off the oil supply to the big ends, leading to seizure. A crowded roller bearing substitute was felt to be uneconomical – but it surely would not have been as costly as the warranty claims would be. The factory sidecar race engines developed an end-fed

The 654cc engine was over square at 75 x74mm, and that contributed to the notorious vibration of these twins. Another factor may have been their all-welded frames, which soaked up the shakes less well than brazed-lug chassis with bolted-on rear sub-frames, like the Triumphs. US variants suffered worst, as they were often geared down for improved acceleration. Whatever the cause, the results when you pressed on were indisputable. Road testers tiptoed round this with words like 'annoying', but as Mike Clay put it, "For vibration, they rated among the worst parallel twins, and that really is saying something."

With all this, as a touring and general-purpose bike the unit BSA could settle down, as the mileage mounted, to be a pleasant enough ride (though never quite as pleasant as the pre-units). They leaked oil less, started easily, and at real-world speeds could be tireless, with useful power. A 1965 Rider's Report in Motor Cycle magazine found the front end, still with only rebound damping, could wallow at speed on bumpy bends, the

ABOVE *Rockers did not care for BSA unit twins, but this 1965 Lightning looks OK.*

RIGHT *Twins on a twin in this November 1961 advertisement.*

Introduced late in 1962, the unit twins' styling was part of Edward Turner's efforts to make motorcycles smoother and more socially acceptable, reversing rockers like Clay's negative impact, as scooters had. Eighteen-inch wheels all round enforced this. The BSA escaped rear panelling but the bulbous steel side-panels were designed to hide the empty space freed up by the lack of a magneto. And they also covered up 'mechanicals', in this case the carburettor(s). It was not appreciated. Weighing in at 390lb the A65 Star was some 30lb lighter than the pre-units, but it did not look it.

BRUMMAGEM DRAY

The engine layout echoed the pre-unit's, with a gear-driven single camshaft to the rear of the cylinder. Main bearings were now a ball journal on the drive side, but on

crank solution, but even when the A65 briefly went to 750cc towards the end, the plain bush stayed.

The gearbox and its four-spring clutch echoed the Triumph's, as Turner aimed for commonality of group components. It thus had a Triumph-type, down-for-first shift pattern. A good-breathing cylinder head with large, well-positioned valves, and an inlet manifold easily adaptable for twin carburettors, promised much tuning potential for the initial single carb tourer. The US-oriented triplex primary drive chain signalled this was going to be exploited across the water.

clutch could slip, and the gearbox give problems. But overall, they gave these early unit twins, as you hoped for from a BSA, a 92% rating for reliability.

LIGHTNING

With the American market opening up, it was they who got the first twin carb A65, the 1964 Lightning Rocket. It featured

ABOVE AND ABOVE RIGHT *A 1965 A65LC Lightning Clubmans 650. Siamesed exhaust, racing seat, Ace bars and rear-sets.*

a sports camshaft, a brace of 1 1/8in Monobloc carburettors, and a 109mph top end.

The A65's breakout year was 1965. The twin carb A65L Lightning was released in the UK, with a revised frame, along with 360 Lightning Clubmans production racers. The top 650cc twins' appearance had been transformed. There were chromed blade mudguards, a chromed top shroud for the gaitered front forks, a separate chromed headlamp, twinned instruments, and sculpted fibreglass side-panels, cut back to expose the carburettors. With a 3.25 x 19in front wheel and a 4.00 x 18 rear, plus a red-lined metallic gold paint finish, the 48bhp Lightning was quite spectacular-looking.

It featured as SPECTRE's rocket-firing steed in James Bond's 'Thunderball', apparently ridden by Luciana Paluzzi. Sidecar

champion Chris Vincent was going to be her stunt double, but scheduling delays meant that it was a movie professional, Johnny Walker, who fired the rockets into the target Lincoln for real, and swerved off at close to 100mph to get clear of the explosion's debris.

At Silverstone that year, BSA hired Mike Hailwood to contest a 15-lap production race on a Lightning Clubmans. The A65LC Clubmans featured a siamesed exhaust, a racing seat with a rearward-facing red Gold Star badge on its seat hump, dropped Ace bars, a close-ratio gearbox, and a claimed 51bhp output. Having won the meeting's 350cc and 500cc races, Hailwood in pouring rain diced with the Triumphs of Phil Read and Percy Tait, to take the flag.

Sadly, the Clubmans did not do so well in the 500-mile production races, often going down to the prevalent 'rogue spark'. This was due to the Lucas 4CA's unsuitable contact-breaker cam, causing high engine temperatures, sticking valves, and piston failures. JoMo's Pete Colman was often credited with solving the problem, but in fact this was done via painstaking work by Meriden's Frank Baker. The A65LC did not enjoy the Thruxton Bonneville's success, but it provided a model for the moment when the A65's image turned from cosy commuter to scorching road burner.

BAD BOYS

In 1966 the sports A65 became the Spitfire Mk II, a charismatic, 120mph fire-breather, but a troublesome machine on the road. This was due to that year's unsuitable racing Amal

LEFT *Mike Hailwood on a A65LC riding to victory in a 1965 Silverstone production race.*

GP carburettors, and to truly severe vibration. John 'Mooneyes' Cooper won that year's Hutchinson 100 race on one.

In America, the race news was not so good. Confined to 500cc in competition by the AMA rules, Harry Sturgeon authorised four special A50s to be sent to Daytona at the same time as Hele's Meriden T100s. The BSAs featured special frames, magnesium crankcases, clutches turned from solid dural shaft, and had all

petrol tank with bigger chrome areas, the shape showing off the finned cover nicely. The tank also carried new anodised alloy badges, less prone to splitting from the vibration. Concentric carburettors came in, and 6CA contact breakers plus an RM21 alternator were positive improvements.

However, the twin leading shoe front brakes were Triumph improvements. So would be 1969's shorter forks to cure front

away, for 1969 introducing a redesigned frame with a 32in seat height. They also widened the crankcase and primary chain case joint faces by 15%, to counter oil leaks.

But the American magazines were frank. "For years," said 'Cycle', "BSA was the worst offender (among the big manufacturers), shipping bikes with parts not tightened or adjusted properly; with electrical wiring that could short-circuit; with poor quality

ABOVE *US styling on these 1968 A65s on the production track at Small Heath.*

ABOVE *Chris Vincent on the rocket firing A65LC from 1965 Bond movie Thunderball.*

the phosphor bronze bearings replaced with needle rollers.

But three of the four failed to finish, due to ignition trouble. The machines were using ET (Energy Transfer) battery-less ignition, originally developed by Lucas for other applications. This time it was Pete Colman who had found how to make the system reliable. The winning T100s were similarly equipped, so it looks as though Pete was not sharing. The following year saw six more special A50s entered, but all six failed to finish.

BSA didn't give up on the A65's appearance or tweaking the engineering. In 1966 the drive-side main switched from ball to roller bearings, and a thrust washer was inserted between the timing side bush and the crankshaft web. Bigger carbs and lower gearing for the A65L ramped up acceleration for the standing ¼ mile and there was a first attempt at front fork damping, to cure the front-end handling problems.

A handsome finned rocker cover was introduced for 1967, replacing the previous bland plain top. But US Triumph dealers and riders still referred scornfully to the unit twins with their oval engine covers as 'the water-melon engine'. Twelve months later, 1968 brought the US export styling for all, including a curved 2¾ gallon

ABOVE *A 1966 A65SS Spitfire Mk II, with GP carbs and optional five-gallon fibreglass tank.*

end lightness, with their genuinely two-way damped internals, and 1970's three-ball-and-ramp clutch mechanism. Meriden had the engineering edge. Before that there had been another expensive BSA blind alley, attempting to convert A65 engines to overhead camshafts. The engineer involved, Martin Russell, later stated bluntly that "the A65 didn't need an overhead cam, it needed a decent bottom end."

With the Rocket 3 coming, 1968's A65SS Spitfire Mk IV was the last year for the twin as BSA's flagship. With the A65 still their major seller, Small Heath beavered

gaskets that would permit the engine to leak oil," adding that some "dealers would not take the trouble to prep a BSA thoroughly." This was in 1971, and a preliminary to praising improvements. But by then it was too late.

TO DRAWING

Yet the great US racer Dick Mann, who campaigned the unit twins from 1969, wrote of the A65, "That was a great racing engine. All you needed was a set of Carillo rods, a HY-Vo primary chain, a little headwork on the ports and valves."

ABOVE *Carefully built A65 Lightning engine + Featherbed frame special = serious fun.*

He came sixth on BSAs in the AMA National Championship ratings. While the pre-1969 rules had enforced the use of the A50, it could not compete with the lighter 500cc Triumphs. It was the same in the desert with the 500cc Wasp and 650cc Hornet scramblers. The BSA engine was wider and heavier, at 135lb, than the Triumph's. After the rule change, Mann, Jim Rice and Dave Aldana did well on the dirt-tracks with the A65, and with BSA's answer to the T120RT, the 200 homologated 750cc A70 twins.

By the end in 1972, some 58,000 A50 and A65s had been built. What was the secret to a good one? Sidecar champion Chris Vincent said that at Small Heath he could sight up castings and pick ones off the line so that he could grade and control cylinder heads, con rods, cranks, cylinders and pistons, and operators would machine them to the tighter tolerances he wanted.

Steve Mettam, a stylist at Umberslade Hall, provided a further insight on an A65F Firebird street scrambler he used

ABOVE *Take it steady and A65s like this 1968 single carb Thunderbolt could be a nice ride.*

LEFT *Handsome. An A50 Royal Star from 1970, the final year of 500cc manufacture.*

there. It was remarkably tractable, yet when he opened the throttle, amazing. The former-Small Heath operator who had built it up explained: "It was to drawing." He said the factory always took short-cuts, never machining the cylinder heads exactly to the drawings. Part of the cutting operation was never completed; the heads were used 'as cast'. "This is the first one other than racing machines to be machined to drawings." It put out 58bhp and would wheelie without slipping the clutch. "A65s 'to drawing,'" Mettam concluded, "would have impressed their owners if they had ever hit the street!"

The Hybrids
FAST PARTNERS

BEFORE THE ARRIVAL OF THE BEST-SELLING COMMANDO, US DEMAND PRODUCED SOME FINAL SEXY MASHUPS FOR AMC.

The Atlas-engined Norton/Matchless hybrids' origins went back to the mid-1950s and extended forward to 1969. They were only ever built in limited numbers, but punched above their weight in terms of charisma, truly thrilling performance, and as link models to the upcoming Commando.

The story began with Norton in Bracebridge Street. In early 1958, to satisfy a US order, a twin engine, the relatively new 600cc, was slotted into a pre-Featherbed Norton frame, and tweaked with twin carbs to give 36bhp against the stock 31bhp. Dubbed the Norton Nomad, with lightened cycle parts such as alloy mudguards and a siamesed exhaust, but still heavy at 400lb, these were sent out for desert racing. Their pale seat tops indicated this, though with full lights they were really

dual-purpose machines. That would be a feature of the hybrids to come. Some 200 Nomads were exported until 1960.

Why were the peerless, and lighter, Featherbed frames not deployed? It had been found with early examples that even when bumping a Featherbed Norton up over a kerb, the headstock arrangement did not provide enough support and the front forks could be pushed back. That was cured by adding a bracing gusset at the headstock. But in combination with bars featuring a quite restricted steering lock, the Featherbed was not suitable for withstanding off-road shocks.

THE SINGLE STRAND
Meanwhile, Matchless had also been exporting machines, in their case heavyweight singles, for American competition.
From 1955

the 500cc Matchless G80R featured a rigid rear end and a modern front. Bud Ekins, future Triumph star and 'The Great Escape' stunt double for his friend Steve McQueen, had successfully campaigned off-road on Matchless in the early 1950s.

A 1964 cross-country Matchless scrambler, never listed in the UK, was the G80TCS Typhoon. It had first been put together by the then West Coast AMC importer Frank Cooper, with the standard late short-stroke G80's 86x85.5mm dimensions enlarged to 89x96mm to give 596cc. After a bottom end redesign for 1964, incorporating the Norton oil pump, the existing, fairly successful but heavy G80CS scrambler, was displaced for 1965.

By then Matchless were up against both the two-strokes and the highly-successful, Rickman Metisse-framed specials built with Triumph engines.

ABOVE This 1965 G85CS scrambler is one half of the ultimate hybrid.

The Rickman frame weighed in at just 28lb. AMC more or less copied the Rickman chassis to create the G85CS, though theirs was not oil-bearing. It was a duplex downtube frame in Reynolds 531, with an AJS 7R conical rear hub and a front one lightened by machining off its fins. With a central alloy oil tank and a 2.2 gallon red fibreglass petrol tank, the claimed weight was 291lb, though according to off-road expert Don Morley, the actual figure was 318lb.

That was still 27lb lighter than the G80CS, and the engine as sold produced 42 bhp. But at 71mph with scrambles gearing, the G85CS was not particularly fast, and with a massive GP carburettor, not that flexible either. The G85CS, as the twins would be, was sometimes badged as a Norton, sometimes as a Matchless.

GROUND-SHAKIN'

Meanwhile, Norton twins were back in the desert hunt, with the late 1963 Norton Atlas Scrambler. The 750cc twin was fitted in a hearth-brazed Matchless frame with its forged head-lug. The scrambler was produced at the request of AMC's new US distributor, Joe Berliner. A Hungarian survivor of a Nazi concentration camp, Joe and his brother Michael set up the Berliner Motor Corps in Hasbrouck Heights, New Jersey in 1957. As well as introducing the Ducati marque to America, they increasingly dictated what AMC built. In 1964 the company, operating at a loss, had been forced to mortgage the Plumstead works, just to be able to fulfil a large order for singles to Czechoslovakia. Berliner was in fact in negotiations to buy AMC in 1966 when the receivers were called in.

The thundering 750cc Atlas Scrambler, coded N15CS (N), was a dual-purpose version of what would be the 1965 Matchless G15/AJS Model 33 roadsters, as the twins adopted the Norton front end and engine, with AMC's alloy primary chain case cover replacing Norton's pressed steel version. A production run of 200 of the scramblers were shipped out and they proved successful, with top rider Mike Patrick taking the number one plate for 1964 in the Mojave desert. With low-level uptilted open pipes, a 2.2 gallon alloy gas tank and special Girling rear shocks which would continue on the other Hybrids, the scramblers put out 49bhp in stock form.

The importer also noted that several customers replaced the scrambler's knobbly tyres with road ones, and

RIGHT The P11A Ranger with gold-lined tank and uptilted silencers that cost a couple of horse power but made the beast road-legal.

found them just as impressive when used as a street bike. A batch of 95 G15 CSR street scramblers, with low level exhausts and Norton silencers, were also later despatched. Between 1965 and 1967, over 2,000 G15 CS street scrambler variants would be built. If enthusiast customers preferred the Norton to the Matchless name, it was simply a matter of the dealer unscrewing the tank badges and exchanging them. Custom Rodder magazine described the Atlas Scrambler as "The Hottest of the Hot Cycles." And there was more to come.

THE CHEETAH 45

AMC went under in August 1966 and was absorbed into Dennis Poore's Norton-Villiers. Berliner was still their US importer and continued to look for a marketable product that could be made from what was left at Plumstead, which was now under a compulsory purchase order issued by the local council.

The N15CS (N) with its extended Norton forks was good and sold reasonably well, but for the desert it was heavy at 410lb, against the 364lb Triumph TR6. It was Berliner who suggested to his west coast representative, Bob Blair of ZDS Motors, that the Atlas engine could go in the G85CS single's cycle parts, which included late Matchless long-travel forks from the 1963 650cc CSR, with the modified, lighter seven-inch front brake. Blair, who was heavily involved in the 200-mile Mojave desert races, promptly shoe-horned two of the modified Atlas motors into G85CS frames, and sent one back to Plumstead.

The new model, which was announced in March 1967 as the P11, for export only, was not popular with Plumstead's fitters, or with management. It was a tricky job to marry the frame and engine, involving a lot of spacers - which were never to be documented in a parts book. There were many separate engine mounting spacers, resulting in the danger of parts loosening if not really tightened up. If the spacers were not positioned correctly, chain alignments would not be true, and this could damage chaincases and other components. If incorrectly positioned, the prop-stand lug could damage the thin-walled Reynolds 531 frame.

Memphis dealer Leo Goff was told that P11s were always unprofitable for the factory, as they were so labour-intensive – you could assemble three Commandos in the time it took to do just one P11. Yes, Commandos, for just six months after the P11's debut came the launch of Norton's 750cc Commando. From then on, the hybrid's days were numbered.

The P11 differed from the Atlas in fitting dual 930 Concentric carburettors not Monoblocs, and coil ignition rather than a magneto – but the sting was taken out of that by the presence of a new Lucas capacitor system, developed for the ISDT, which allowed reliable battery-less starting and running. The P11 had a camshaft designed to deliver more torque, and this it certainly did. The handlebars were high, wide, cross-braced and well-positioned.

For the end user, this big, lean twin delivered the goods. Weighing in at just 366lb, these Nortons beat out the Triumphs to take the number one Mojave plate for the two years of their production. With only slightly lower gearing than the stock G15 roadster – the same 19T gearbox sprocket was still in place – but with 8 ½ inches of ground clearance, a long 57½in wheelbase for straight-line blasting, putting out 52.5bhp at 6,400 rpm and good for 110mph, for a while these hairy beasts truly kicked sand in the face of the opposition.

But the majority of buyers changed tyres, as most of the scramblers, with their lean looks and candy-apple red paint jobs on the 2.2 gallon tanks, were used as road bikes, blasting down the

BELOW *A later P11A, with an altered, unlined tank and longer seat. Some kept high pipes, some not.*

BELOW *Some called the P11 prehistoric. Get one on the road and find out for yourself.*

ABOVE *A P11, the earliest type from 1967. Note the small seat and no rear chain guard.*

ABOVE *A young Clint Eastwood astride a Ranger in London. Wonder where he stored the road atlas?*

highway. They delivered phenomenal, breath-taking, addictive acceleration at the twist of the grip. One journalist wrote, "As the hedgerows blurred and the rev counter passed the 5,000 rpm mark, a feeling of fantastic exhilaration surged up as you held everything together with the throttle." A light front end, a squirming rear, the answer was the same – throttle on!

The P11 came in three phases. There were some problems with the early ones, which wore high pipes with the kind of beautiful compound bends that were Plumstead's pride. But dealer Lee Cowie described them as "scientifically developed high exhaust pipes down each side, so no matter how you tried, you could not help but burn yourself." He also believed that the oil tanks had not been fully tested, as they split all too easily, and the P11 became known as "the Peeled Lemon." Maybe that was why the importers also dubbed it the 'Cheetah 45' (45 cu in is the US equivalent of 750cc.)

This was remedied early in 1968 with the P11A, which tacitly acknowledged the majority use as street scramblers. It featured low, uptilted pipes which cost two bhp, and a successfully modified oil tank mounting. It fitted the same polished alloy guards as the earlier ones, but the red tanks, still with the circular plastic badges, were no longer lined in silver. The final act in the autumn of 1968, was the P11 Ranger, another low-pipe model, this time with transfers not badges on the tank, which became gold-lined. It also fitted a different seat, similar to that on the G80CS, and chromed steel mudguards. This swansong was more 'street' than 'scrambler'.

The P11 hybrids were scarcely a practical roadster, with the later Ranger variants a little better. The brakes weren't really up to its speed, and the handling on high speed corners was described as "notably approximate." You got wet on the high-pipe ones because you couldn't wear over-trousers without the pipes melting them, the noise was

definitely for wide open spaces not built-up areas, and vibration could be bad enough to shake their lighting systems off and split their seats.

But still… one rider described the Ranger as "like a living thing beneath you – things felt as if they could go either way any minute, and this living on the edge was such a blast." As *Cycle World* summed up the 1967 P11: "they may be a bit heavy, and their packaging more than a little old-fashioned, but these fabulous Nortons will still give you rides as exhilarating as any you're likely to experience."

They were to be the last hybrid, with some 2,500 P11/Ranger models built in all. But their influence on Norton looks and style was to be profound. The 2.2 gallon tank, chopped alloy mudguards, high level or upswept exhaust systems, and overall aggressively minimal styling would soon resurface in the Roadster and 750SS versions of the Commando – and the Roadster was to be the best-selling variant of them all.

Three
OF A KIND

WITH THE IMPENDING THREAT FROM JAPANESE MANUFACTURERS, THE BSA GROUP LOOKED TO TRIPLES TO STAY IN THE RACE.

ABOVE *Jeff Smith on Rocket 3 (Left) with one-time James Bond George Lazenby on Trident. But Lazenby bought the BSA, reg. POP 950G*

ABOVE *A publicity shot of a 1969 Rocket 3 in Blackpool. Not Santa Monica, but it would do.*

Launched in September 1968, just two weeks before the 750 Honda-Four, the BSA A75R Rocket 3 and the Triumph Trident T150 had been "conceived at the right time," as author Dave Sheehan put it, "but born too late."

Details of the delays in the triples' gestation period can be found in the chapter beginning on page 18, A Decade of Success. The costly decision to manufacture them as two distinct models was also down to company politics, both at home and in the US.

It had been the BSA Group as well who had dictated that the triples should look decidedly different from the twins. Styling was handed over to design consultants Ogle. Mockers point out that one of their previous projects had been the Reliant Robin three-wheeler given the nickname the 'Plastic Pig', though Ogle had also laid out the quite smart Reliant Scimitar sports car. However, they had styled no motorcycles.

The brief given to two young stylists was to go for "a very flashy American look, like a Cadillac car." BSA on their version also required everything to be angled forward, and this was duly done, with the Rocket 3's 4.25-gallon fuel tank and side panels, all in Ogle's boxy modern style, slanting forward. The BSA's cylinders sloped forward at 15°, while the Tridents were upright.

Meriden designer Doug Hele was appalled at the results, which as Bert Hopwood observed had been further "minced about" at Umberslade Hall. East Coast BSA's Don Brown was also horrified. The silencers, with their three tiny tailpipes, were a sticking point, felt to be more appropriate to a scooter. One older US executive liked the 'ray-gun' silencers, as they came to be known, because they reminded him of pre-war Velocette 'fish-tail' ones.

This was ironic, as Ogle had adhered to Hele's instructions to leave plenty of volume inside whatever they came up with. Doug then designed efficient baffling inside the ray-guns, based on Velocette reverse flow practice. The triples always went best with ray-guns, so long as the airbox used with them originally was also fitted. Their nerve-tingling yowl at race speed was to be a triple trademark.

OLD STYLE

The ohv engine design was more Triumph than BSA, with fore and aft camshafts, driven by gears and operating pushrods in vertical tubes lying between the cylinders. All that was as on Meriden's twins. The cylinder dimensions at 67x70mm were those of the BSA/Triumph unit singles. Compression ratio was 9.5:1, and capacity 740cc.

The heart of these machines was the forged crankshaft. After the initial forging, this was re-heated and skilfully twisted to give the 120° crank throw. Balance was by the shaft's internal webs, with no flywheel fitted. Hele had been concerned about possible vibration from the three-cylinder layout, due to differing thicknesses of the crank webs. Small Heath, where all the engines would be built, invested £80,000 in a German grinding machine to solve this problem.

Though manufacturing the crank was a time-consuming process, the result was outstanding. The crank could cope with outputs which rose from the first roadsters' 58bhp at 7,250rpm, to an eventual 85bhp on the racers.

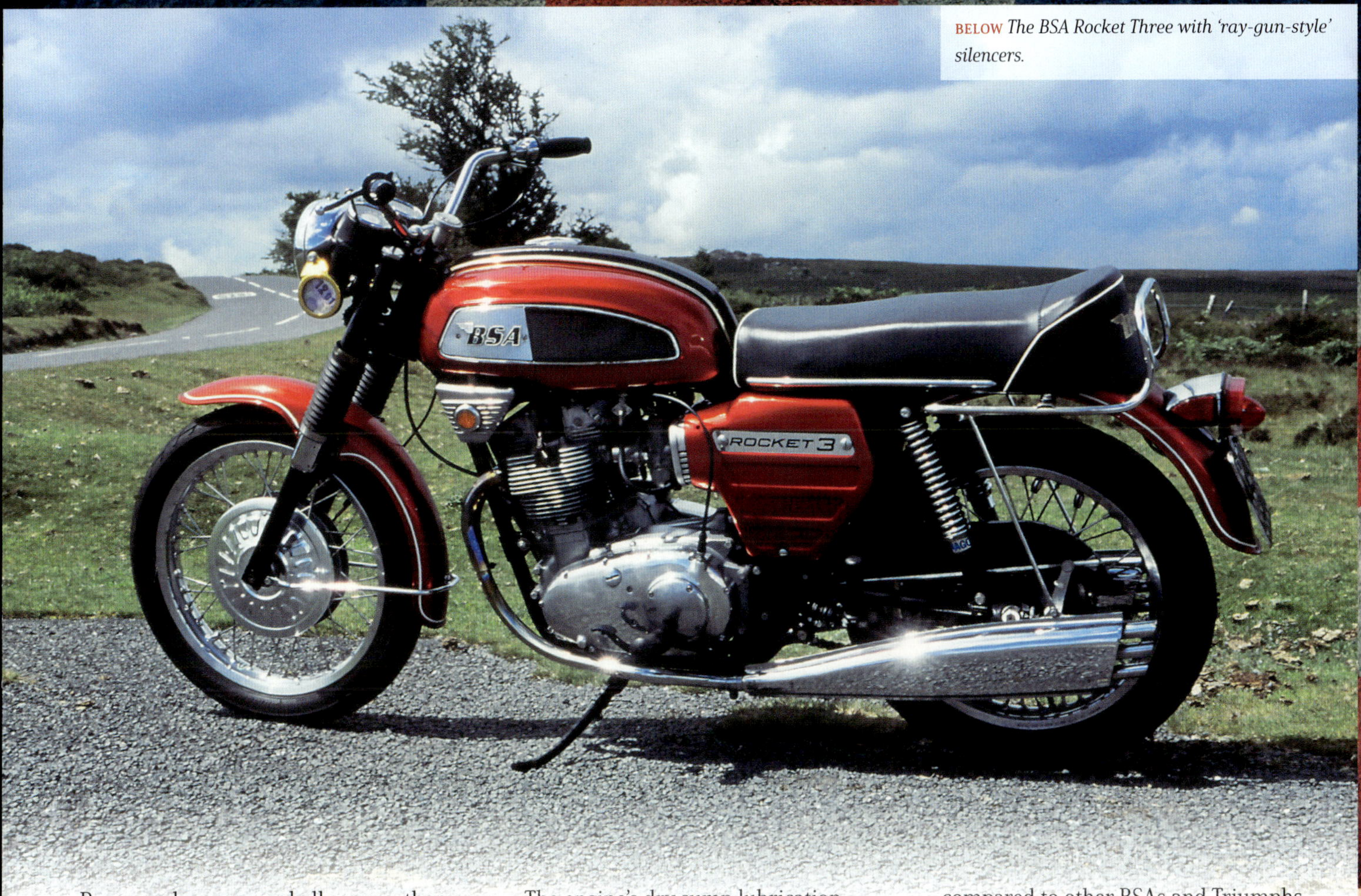

BELOW *The BSA Rocket Three with 'ray-gun-style' silencers.*

Race cranks were used all season, then re-ground and used again. As Jack Shemans of Meriden Experimental wrote: "The Trident crankshaft is the strongest in any motorcycle engine and has never been known to break." This un-burstable bottom end meant that the motor could be safely revved beyond the 7,400rpm limit.

The engine's dry sump lubrication system was conventional, but the oil from the six-pint tank was circulated three and a half times faster than in a 650cc twin, thanks to a new, double-plunger pump. A 1/4-pint capacity oil cooler also sat under the tank nose. It benefited the semi-obscured middle cylinder in particular. Leaks on this engine were reduced, compared to other BSAs and Triumphs.

The crankshaft ran on four bearings, two plain middle ones, lubricated by pressure-feed, plus drive side ball and timing side roller bearings. The alternator sat, unusually, on the right, timing side end of the crankshaft. This kept it out of the hot, oily primary chaincase, and saved space, meaning that the triple engine was only 3½in wider than the 650cc Triumph twin.

The shaft was carried in a three-piece, vertically split aluminium alloy crankcase, since tooling-up for horizontally split, leak-proof Japanese-style cases was not an option. Making the centre section of the engine/gearbox shell involved 56 different operations using 46 jigs. The bottom of the engine was built up from seven different castings, and as works manager Al Cave observed, making it all oil-tight was "laborious."

Cave added that "an incredible amount of time was wasted changing machines over from one version" (the upright Trident) "to the other" (the Rocket 3 with cylinder slanted forward 15°) "and back again." The cases differed too, with the Triumphs', as on their unit twin, machined to show the shape of their two distinct timing chest and gearbox portions. The BSA's was a single flowing shape. Another delaying factor

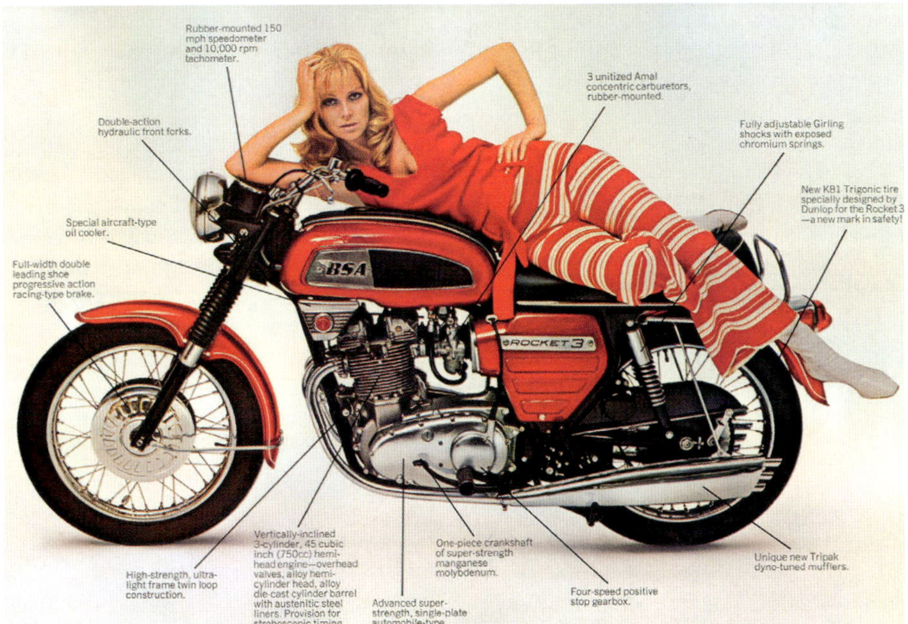

BELOW *The T150 Trident.*

ABOVE RIGHT *For racing, it had to be the ray-gun silencers.*

RIGHT *The heavily finned BSA three-cylinder 750cc all-alloy engine.*

was that each cylinder in the heavily finned alloy block, all three topped by a single alloy head, had to be bored individually. Hele was incredulous, as he had seen multi-boring as an apprentice with Austin in the 1930s!

The result of all this was initial engine production of just 50 a week. This would increase marginally, when the Small Heath forge was closed in 1970 and the work contracted out to motor component specialists Garringtons in Bromsgrove. Meriden as well as Small Heath would have production lines for the complete machines. But annual triple production was limited by the engine issues to no more than 7,000 machines a year.

It took an American executive, Don Brown, to point this out to the group MD Eric Turner. He also made it clear to the boss that the triples' styling and high price were undoubtedly going to limit sales. Reportedly, Eric Turner was stunned to realise that the machine which the group had been pinning their hopes on could never be profitably produced. The board had been hoping to see a return on their triple tooling investment in a totally unrealistic one year.

The lack of economies of scale due to relatively limited production, meant that the triple's price was noticeably high. This was a further point against it, along with the unusual styling. The first models had gone to the US, but when they reached the UK in April 1969, the Rocket 3 cost £614,

when a 750cc Norton Commando S cost £525. In 1969 around 7,000 of the triples were sold. That year's figure for the new 750 Honda-Four, with disc brake, five-speed gearbox, overhead cam engine and electric start, was 30,000 units.

DIFFERENT STROKES

The chassis for BSA and Triumph triples were different. BSA favoured the all-welded, duplex downtube type as found on their twins. Meriden stuck with their traditional style which featured a single downtube and brazed-lug construction with bolted-up rear sub-frame. The BSA version had a wheelbase 1¾in shorter than the Triumph. There was little to choose between the handling, though a *Motor Cycle* rider's report thought the BSA had a slight edge. A 1968 *Cycle World* T150 test felt that riders accustomed to the lighter twins might find the Three's

handling "cumbersome and deliberate" in comparison, and that it wasn't for footpeg-scraping – "the bike just does not inspire in its riders that much confidence." And that was riding on the new Dunlop K81/TT100 tyres.

It was true that triples were a different ballgame. At 468lb dry, they were 70lb heavier than even an equivalent Norton Commando. And triple ground clearance was poor enough to limit cornering. The steering was necessarily heavy rather than nimble, requiring the bike to be put into corners deliberately. But the handling and roadholding were fundamentally sound and stable, with the engine weight being well forward contributing to a firm footprint. And more than one rider commented on how the good mid-range power pulled you out of trouble if you went too deep on bends.

BELOW *A BSA triple racer with a Rob North-style frame.*

In the same vein, triples were not as torquey as twins, and accelerated smoothly rather than arm-wrenchingly. This lack of bottom end could be masked partially by lower gearing, but that made the already poor fuel consumption figures even worse. The triples needed more revs than a traditional twin, but once you were in the zone, ran further and faster than the latter, with speeds in the four gears 50, 80, 110, and 125mph. And when the Yanks really turned up the wick, a Trident could go from 0 to 60 in just five seconds, nearly a second faster than a T120R Bonneville. The relative lack of vibration meant you could maintain high speeds over long distances. The only very occasional limitation was the rear chains available at the time then letting go in prolonged, repeated high speed highway runs.

TEETHING TROUBLES

However, things did not begin well. There was a rash of serious engine failures. Hele despatched Meriden Experimental trouble-shooter Alan Barrett to California, where hundreds of T150s awaited sale. Barrett found swarf in carburettors, seized pistons, misaligned threads on alternators, incorrect cam timing, and poorly punched holes in oil pump gaskets blocking oil feed.

Bert Hopwood at Meriden put Barrett and a team into Small Heath, where there was more. The primary chainwheels had sometimes been misaligned, which could lead to the triplex chains snapping and damaging the crankshaft. It was traced to the chainwheels having been made out of line. The operative machining them had been putting three and even six at a time on his broaching machine, to get his piecework money up.

The triple contact breakers were found to sometimes have been poorly

BELOW *The 1971 Rocket 3 Mk 2, part of BSA's new range. The megaphone silencers looked good but were no improvement.*

ABOVE *Part of a brochure for the 1969 Rocket 3, California dreaming.*

RIGHT *A T160 Trident on track, with aftermarket double discs and Norton-type 'peashooter' silencers.*

adjusted, which could lead to holed pistons. Tracing erratic tickover, it was found that the Lucas automatic advance/retard mechanisms were fitted with light springs which allowed the timing to wander. Replacing them with heavier springs was tried, but that tended to retard the ignition too much at high rpm. The eventual answer was to be one heavy and one light spring.

BAD VIBRATIONS

One of the worst early troubles was the return of punishing vibration on some but not all triples. Hele investigated and found that someone at the factory had come up with a bright idea to speed up the machining of the crankshaft, which had sometimes upset the balance factor.

This ceased forthwith, and after their hasty release, the 1969 models got 24 improvements, including stronger con rods, a revised gearbox, and alterations to the primary chain tensioner. The latter would still always require regular attention, or the flapping chain would eventually break the tensioner and put snatch loads on the clutch sprocket, which could snap its rivets.

Gradually things improved. Meanwhile, back in the USA, in April 1969 Don Brown took four production Rocket 3s straight from the crate to break records at Daytona. Pete Colman had disapproved, but chairman Lionel Jofeh himself had given the go-ahead, as it might boost BSA over Triumph. The triples averaged 127mph for an hour, and 123.4mph for 200 miles.

French Canadian racer Yvon Duhamel over five miles from a flying start averaged 131.7mph. This broke AMA records, and over 50 years ago, was amazing from a stock production motorcycle. Production racing victories were being achieved in the UK and Europe too.

BSA/Triumph had sold 7,510 triples for 1969, despite continuing resistance to the slab-sided looks. Texan Big D's Jack Wilson had said: "We couldn't give those '69 Tridents away they were so ugly." And then – production fell to between 400 and 500 triples in total for the whole of 1970. They had a model that was just coming good, emphasized by Hele's Rob North-framed works racers second and third placing at Daytona, the fruits of a $1 million race effort – and then failed

BELOW *The T160 Trident, last of the line*

to produce that model to capitalize on the expensive victory. The reason was the chaotic preparations for the 1971 range, and Jofeh's costly and disruptive internal reorganization of Small Heath itself.

BEAUTY KIT

For 1970, the triple's joint faces were increased by 15% to help oil-tightness. The US export machines had their overall gearing lowered. The lubrication system was improved. In response to continuous feedback about sales resistance to the styling, from early in 1971 Tridents were issued with a 'beauty kit' which made

designed factory custom, the spectacular X75 Hurricane. It had originally been commissioned by Don Brown as a BSA and used the Rocket 3's forward-angled engine.

REAL WORLD

For the owner, pre-1971 Rocket 3s and T150s required dedication. The 9.5:1 compression ratio engine was at least easy to start, but troubles remained to counter the speed and power. The drum brakes were limiting, the rear one poor and the front one, though excellent, not up to the 120mph plus performance. The Borg and Beck diaphragm clutch, used in the

mind, wrote that "A Three renews one's faith in motorcycles and motorcycling… When you are riding one you don't want to stop riding."

The ongoing triple saga continued, with Hele's genius achieving race success against the odds and the rising tide of Japanese two-strokes. In competition, only on the US dirt did they fail to thrive. Top triple racer Jim Rice wrote that on mile tracks, "The three-cylinder was slightly slower than a twin on the straightaways, and more difficult in the turns because of increased engine width. The primary dragged the ground when the motorcycle

The BSA Rocket 3 had presence.

them look like Triumph twins. Jack Wilson celebrated by taking a sledgehammer to 30 of the old slab-sided gas tanks. One unfortunate new feature was the megaphone-style silencers, which did not give the performance yield of the ray-guns. Trident sales in 1972 and 1973 became healthy, though still limited by the number of engines that could be made.

In 1971 BSA had come out with the Rocket 3 Mk 2, featuring the new range's pale frame, slim front forks, new (even worse) drum brakes with conical hubs, and like the restyled Tridents, a 2.5 Imperial gallon petrol tank, the BSA's in painted chrome. This gave a potential range of as little as 75 miles. Being narrower, it also let rain in to the three carburettors, where the rod which operated them ran through a wear-prone rubber seal.

The BSA's big tank returned for 1972 along with black frames, but only 641 more Rocket 3s were made before BSA was gone. Meriden sold 6,040 triples in 1973, and that included around 1,200 of the Craig Vetter-

restricted space of a motorcycle chaincase, meant that much of its lifting clearance had to be sacrificed. On the triples it was notoriously short of lift, with the cable requiring constant careful adjustment to avoid clutch slip.

The triples were famously thirsty of both petrol and oil, mpg in the low 40s and a pint of oil every 300 miles being the *good* news. The engine until 1972 suffered from bad valve pocketing as the valve seats were cast iron, and valve guides wore quickly, the tell-tale sign being a smoking exhaust. The rubbers in the clutch sprocket's cush-drive had short lives.

Maintenance every 3,000 miles was both essential and awkward. The exhaust pipes had to come off to remove the sump filter, and most bolts were difficult to access with the necessary torque wrench. Yet fundamentally the triples were more reliable than contemporary twins. And if you were hooked, that was it. The late Cyril Ayton, Editor of *Motor Cycle Sport*, an unobtrusively fast rider with a logical

ABOVE LEFT *A 1973 X75 Triumph Hurricane A Craig Vetter-designed factory custom.*

'ABOVE *Slippery Sam', the legendary uber-successful T150-based production racer.*

was leaned over. This caused both wheels to skate across the track."

But at the Bol d'Or, the Isle of Man, Daytona, in works or production racing form, for a few short years the triple took them all, in a glorious British bike rear-guard action. Eventually, in March 1975 the T160 Trident emerged from the NVT maelstrom, with tilted forward BSA-type cylinders. This allowed an electric start, to go with the five-speed gearbox and disc brakes all round. But the moment had passed. Journalist Mick Duckworth, though a triple fan, finally judged it "a traditional British bike with superbike trimmings tacked on, many of which only just work." The 7,000-odd T160s were the last of around 35,800 triples built between 1968 and 1977.

Norton's
ALL ACTION COMMANDO

THE LAST AND BEST OF ALL THE OLD BRITISH TWINS

By 1968, the 750cc capacity had taken over from 650s as the market leader. Both Bert Hopwood and Doug Hele had been convinced that the vibration inevitable in a 360° parallel twin without a balancer shaft was unacceptable when the capacity was taken to 750cc. But now a 750 emerged, one of the final designs, with the triples, which would give the Japanese a run for their money before the final 1975 collapse of the old British industry.

This was Norton's Commando, a precarious but effective solution to the endemic problem of high-speed vibration, and a wonderful motorcycle to ride. Not for nothing did it come out top in a 1972 US *Cycle* magazine shoot-out with six other bikes, including the latest Japanese, the Honda-Four, and the Trident.

But you had to get a good one.

MAN IN A HURRY

After Dennis Poore had taken over AMC at Plumstead in mid-1966, he was determined to press ahead with a new Norton flagship model, as well as several other projects. One of the latter had been the SPX stepped-piston two-stroke engine being pioneered by Bernard Hooper with his partner John Favill, formerly of BSA and Villiers.

Poore hired them back to Villiers to continue with that. But he also put Hooper to work on the existing Plumstead P10 project, an 800cc dohc twin from ex-Velocette man Charles Udall. But this design, involving three feet of timing chain running in Teflon-lined tubes, was heavy, far from ready, and vibrated badly. Udall also personally antagonised Poore from the start.

Hooper noticed that development work by Plumstead's former Comp shop chief Wally Wyatt, had boosted power from the existing Atlas engine's 49bhp, to a claimed 59bhp, at least the equal of the P10. Poore was demanding, apparently completely unrealistically, that the new model be ready for the September 1967 Show. So, Hooper suggested using the existing Atlas engine but mounting it in a new frame.

Hooper, based at Wolverhampton, had to tackle the problem of Atlas vibration. For at speed, even with lowly 7.5:1 compression, the big Norton was an eyeball-blurring shaker. Hooper could ride but was more of a boffin, but his assistant, the younger Bob Trigg, a former Ariel apprentice who had come from BSA, rode regularly, and put in several practical touches on the project. They worked well together.

Simple rubber mounting had been tried and rejected on the P10. At home, Hooper, sketching, "sleeked a drawing of a Featherbed frame back by angling

BELOW *The early 750cc Fastback Commando mixed old and new styles.*

ABOVE *Note the 'cigar' silencers of the early Fastback.*

LEFT AND RIGHT *An Isolastic mounting, and the later headsteady.*

ABOVE *The Commando was a wild card, all right.*

sketched out one with a massive main spine 2 ¼in diameter x 16-gauge top tube, braced to the steering head.

A one-inch x 16-gauge duplex cradle looped under the engine and rose to points beneath the seat. Struts from the top tube formed a triangulated structure with the rear members of the cradle loop. All stresses were designed to be taken by the top tube and the rear triangulations. The front cradle was said to be an engine mounting convenience. This frame weighed just 24lb, 10lb less than a Featherbed, and represented a significant contribution to the early Commando's overall lightness.

In a meeting at the front downtubes to the rear. Then I cut a photograph of an Atlas engine out of a Norton brochure and stuck it in the frame, tilted forward to match that (frame tube) line."

This broke away from previous Norton twins' severe vertical look, originating with the racing Featherbed and a long history of upright singles. The Commando engine would slope forward (like some of the coming Japanese opposition), and this emphasised its length and grace. The engine's angle was picked up by both the frame tubes and the angle of the rear shock absorbers, imparting a taut, aggressive look. The forward-sloping cylinders would also permit the team to design another, more modern-looking and compact alloy primary chaincase for the engine.

THE PROF

Poore's technical director Dr Stefan Bauer, a former atomic scientist, was head of the project's team. As Hooper said, "*All* his thinking was lateral." Bauer dismissed the Featherbed as "bad engineering" and wanted a frame with as many straight tubes as possible. He had

Plumstead, when the P10 was still under discussion, Hooper made remarks about mounting the swinging-arm on the gearbox, and then laughed at himself. But on the train back to Birmingham, Bob Trigg said it was not such a daft idea. From those discussions the idea grew, and what would be called the Isolastic engine-mounting system developed.

Parallel twins vibrate on a single plane, so the engine, gearbox and swinging arm were to be treated as a single entity, and then coupled to the rest of the frame through rubber mountings whose flexibility existed only within that plane. Including the swinging-arm dealt with the problems of varying chain tension if they had not. At front and rear there were outsize rubber mountings, as well as a headsteady. This was a simple pressing with an S-bend midway, prone to fracture until later replaced with a sprung design. There were also insulating rubbers between the sideplates of the engine mounting and the frame tube, controlling lateral movement of the engine.

MAD MEN

The project then made a further break with tradition. This was still the era when, except for Triumph, a factory's draughtsmen styled its machines. Form followed function, sometimes to the detriment of overall coherent styling. For the Commando, an advertising agency, Wolff Ohlins, was involved, which was not inappropriate for such a breakaway 🇬🇧▶

project. "Some of their suggestions made us laugh," said Hooper, "but others were good."

The initial bike was in the Fastback style, with the seat integrated into a fibreglass tail unit. At the front of the seat, unusual wraparound 'ears' blended into the fibreglass tank and replaced knee-grips. The first bike was all silver, frame included, and the seat orange. There were circular green blobs on the tank and the faces of the twinned instruments, which many did not realise were the new Norton-Villiers corporate logo. Later they were said to be infinity symbols, because that was how long it took to get Norton spares!

The decision to go ahead with the project was only taken in June 1967. Ironically for a motorcycle which would be in production for ten years, in the eyes of its creators and their management, it was a stopgap model, until an overhead cam design came good. Sometimes this had unfortunate effects. The Isolastic mountings had to be adjusted every 5,000 miles by inserting shims to maintain the right amount of movement. Shimming was a laborious process, and Hooper had soon come up with a simpler system of Vernier adjustment. But because the Commando was only expected to be around for a couple of years, the simpler adjustment was shelved on the grounds of expense, until 1975, leaving owners till then with a fiddly, but vital, chore.

Villiers in Wolverhampton were still busy with industrial engines, and in the past had only made motorcycle engines, not whole machines. They were struggling to get the new machine into production in time, and so the project was sent to Plumstead, under designer Tony Denniss and developer Wally Wyatt. Denniss confirmed that "the Commando design was largely done at Wolverhampton under Bernard Hooper." But when three lorry-loads of machines and two Villiers draughtsmen arrived in Woolwich, there was still a lot to do. Denniss' personal agenda was "to bring out a better bike than the Bonneville, and I think we did."

A case in point was the new primary chaincase cover. This was fastened not, as before, by many screws around its periphery, but by a single central fixing bolt, like Royal Enfield's twins. To ensure against leaks if it was overtightened, Denniss had the back end of the chaincase cast so that it tapered outwards and was shallower at each end. This made sure it

would not bow out and leak if the bolt was done up too tightly. When production moved to Wolverhampton in 1973, they ceased to include this feature.

Another thoughtful touch was the seat removal system. On other makes this involved undoing bolts with a spanner. Or with hinged seats, you had to prop them up awkwardly to undertake work or remove the battery. With the Commando, you simply loosened by hand two circular knobs at the top of the suspension units and removed the whole seat. A small touch, but very handy.

SHOW SENSATION

The Commando made it to the 1967 show, and it was a sensation. "No new model introduced in the last decade," wrote tester David Dixon, "has made such a big impact as the Norton Commando." It embodied enough traditional features

ABOVE *The Commando engine was tilted forward to harmonise with frame tubes.*

ABOVE RIGHT *The Wally Wyatt-designed twin leading shoe brake for pre-1972 Commandos.*

RIGHT *A 1972 Fastback, their final year, with Interstate silencers.*

in the engine and cycle parts to reassure enthusiasts, yet with the promise of a breakthrough in terms of frame technology as potentially revolutionary as the Mini. And its style emphasized this without going completely over the top.

On the road, testers were enthusiastic. Despite a high seat and overly forward fixed footrests, *Motor Cycle Mechanics'* man judged a 1968 Fastback "one of the most exciting bikes I have ridden." With 0 – 60 in 4.8 seconds, a standing quarter of 12.8 seconds and a top speed of 122mph, this Norton did not hang about. Early power output was 56bhp, and coupled with a 390lb dry weight, that was thrilling, even before it rose to 60bhp with the use of less restrictive 'peashooter' silencers.

The Commando was an instant hit in the UK, being voted *MCN*'s 'Machine of the Year' five times running. In 1970 the Isolastic system won a Castrol design award of £1,000. Announced a year before the triple and the big Japanese machines, it was the first superbike, brutally good looking, and British.

Between the show and production starting in April 1968, the Atlas clutch was replaced by a diaphragm one, which could be a stiff pull if not set up exactly

ABOVE *Poore commissioned these delightful images and bought the inside front covers of Bike and Cycle World for them.*

ABOVE RIGHT *A 1973 vintage Roadster 750 on the road.*

right and make riding around town a chore. These early machines were a mixture of old and new styles, with familiar gaitered Roadholder forks, and Norton horizontal 'cigar' silencers. They still carried their points/distributor in a compartment behind the cylinder where the old magneto had been positioned.

Wally Wyatt later described the Plumstead production department's resistance to change. He had to get the work done to move the points to the timing chest while the resisters were away from the factory or on holiday. It had not been simple, involving a camshaft redesign to accommodate a re-located rev counter drive. He had already had to go directly to Poore when he discovered that the first 80 Commandos awaiting despatch had been fitted with old Atlas cylinder heads, not the ones he had worked on to produce the extra power. The chairman had intervened, and the new heads had been fitted.

A VERY BRITISH AFFAIR

The Commando was well liked. The new frame, produced like the Featherbed by Reynolds Tubes, might not have handled as sure-footedly as a Featherbed at the highest speeds. A slow weave, known as 'Commando Creep', set in above 90mph, but it was not dangerous. Some felt that the move from the original 3.0x19-inch front and 3.50x 19-inch rear tyres to 4.00 all-round had not helped.

But to riders used to traditional twins, feeling how the shakes disappeared into smoothness once you passed around 2,500 rpm, was quite a transformation. Here was a twin that could handle long rides and motorway runs in relative comfort. The lack of vibration diminished rider fatigue and made ever longer journeys possible.

The lightness, and the separate gearbox's smoother transmission, piled up the points. The 745cc engine with its unfashionably long 90mm stroke kept a lazy, likeable feel to the way the big twin delivered its power. The Commando could go from 0 to 100 in 12 seconds, but its real strength was bottom end stomp, unbelievable torque right from a standstill. The Norton revelled in winding country roads and mountains, where both the torque and the excellent handling in the mid-range could be exploited to the full. While you were doing that, the 1969-on 'peashooter' mufflers gave a lovely crackle, as well as boosting power. The Commando was good in the rain and excellent two-up. In its best year, 1971/72, Norton would sell 17,000 Commandos on both coasts of America.

There were, naturally, troubles big and small. The seven-inch cable-operated rear brake, dictated by the rubber mounting, was ineffective, with a flexing backplate. The Wyatt-designed eight-inch TLS front was, in stock form, not up to BSA/Triumph's, and needed careful work to make it perform adequately. Under the extra power, the shell of the excellent AMC gearbox could flex (before it was strengthened for 1975), and occasionally cause the mainshaft to bow under load, so that gears ran out of true and teeth stripped. But the most common gearbox weak spot was the layshaft bearing. A couple of failures and resulting serious injuries caused the Metropolitan police to abandon their Norton Interpol models.

And right from the launch dealers, mostly in the US, reported frame breakages. They were diagnosed by Reynolds as due to "sudden impact loadings." This was not just Americans at play aviating on the dirt, but crated Commandos, sent from Berliner to dealers, sometimes being dropped bodily, front first, out of the back of a pick-up truck. But five American riders had also been killed, according to Plumstead tester Alan Jones, when they landed badly after jumps and the spindly front downtubes had snapped.

Reynolds expert Ken Sprayson suggested that more was needed than just strengthening the gussets at the steering head, after rigorous testing-to-destruction rides by Plumstead riders over the Army vehicle centre at Chobham. Sprayson said the solution would be to triangulate the bottom of the steering head with a small horizontal bracing tube to a point further down the spine. This cured the problem. Machines were brought back from America to have

RIGHT *One of the last, a Mk V 750, still light and lean, with a front disc from the 850 Mk3.*

ABOVE *An 850cc Interstate Mk 2, a heavier Commando with 'bean-can' silencers to meet noise regulations.*

their frames modified, and this early hiccup was never made public.

Fastbacks, though their looks were rated by many in Europe, did not please everyone in America. So, for 1969 Tony Denniss initiated the S-type. With naked front forks, high 'peashooter' pipes with perforated heat-shields and both running on the left side, a conventional seat, high, wide bars and flamboyant metal-flake paint jobs, in the Easy Rider era they were a magnet to the eye. A particularly striking touch was the chromed ring around the headlamp, potentially to take a stone-guard – a bit of what trainer manufacturers call 'implied performance'.

This was the first of many variants, for in the event, the Commando was to be Norton's only game in town. There was the faux-hippie Hi-Rider, the desert sled SS, the LR, the Interpol, and from 1971, the Roadster, whose small tank and upswept exhaust looks echoed the P11 Ranger. It and the 1972-on Interstate would be the overall best-sellers.

ABOVE *The Commando was popular in Europe. 'La Strider' was the new 1972 Interstate.*

Plumstead closed, prior to demolition, in July 1969. Many considered the Plumstead-built Commandos, sometimes indicated by a 'P' prefix to their engine numbers, the best, despite later improvements. Poore first moved

ABOVE *The Mk V 750, arguably the best Commando*

machine assembly to Andover, where the labour was 'green' compared to the experienced Matchless men. The engines were built in Wolverhampton and trucked down.

After the disastrous 1972 Combat engine fiasco, Poore closed Andover in 1973 and shifted complete manufacture to Wolverhampton. There, production was king, and build standards variable to say the least. The Commando's reliability reputation, already uncertain, never recovered from the Combat episode. This is described in the final Aftermath section, along with the short life and death of NVT. The final Commando 850cc Mk III in 1975 was substantially strengthened, but weighed 466lb dry, and much had been lost.

Seasoned journalist Dave Minton summed up the Commando as "A motorcycle perhaps more than any other, at least in its early days, that provided a truly inspiring ride while gnawing away at its own vitals. Much less from a design flaw than the usual lax production control in British factories…Great bikes, but not good bikes"

The Fall OF BSA

THE ROLLER COASTER RIDE TOWARDS BSA'S DEMISE ACCELERATED WILDLY AS THE 1960S ENDED.

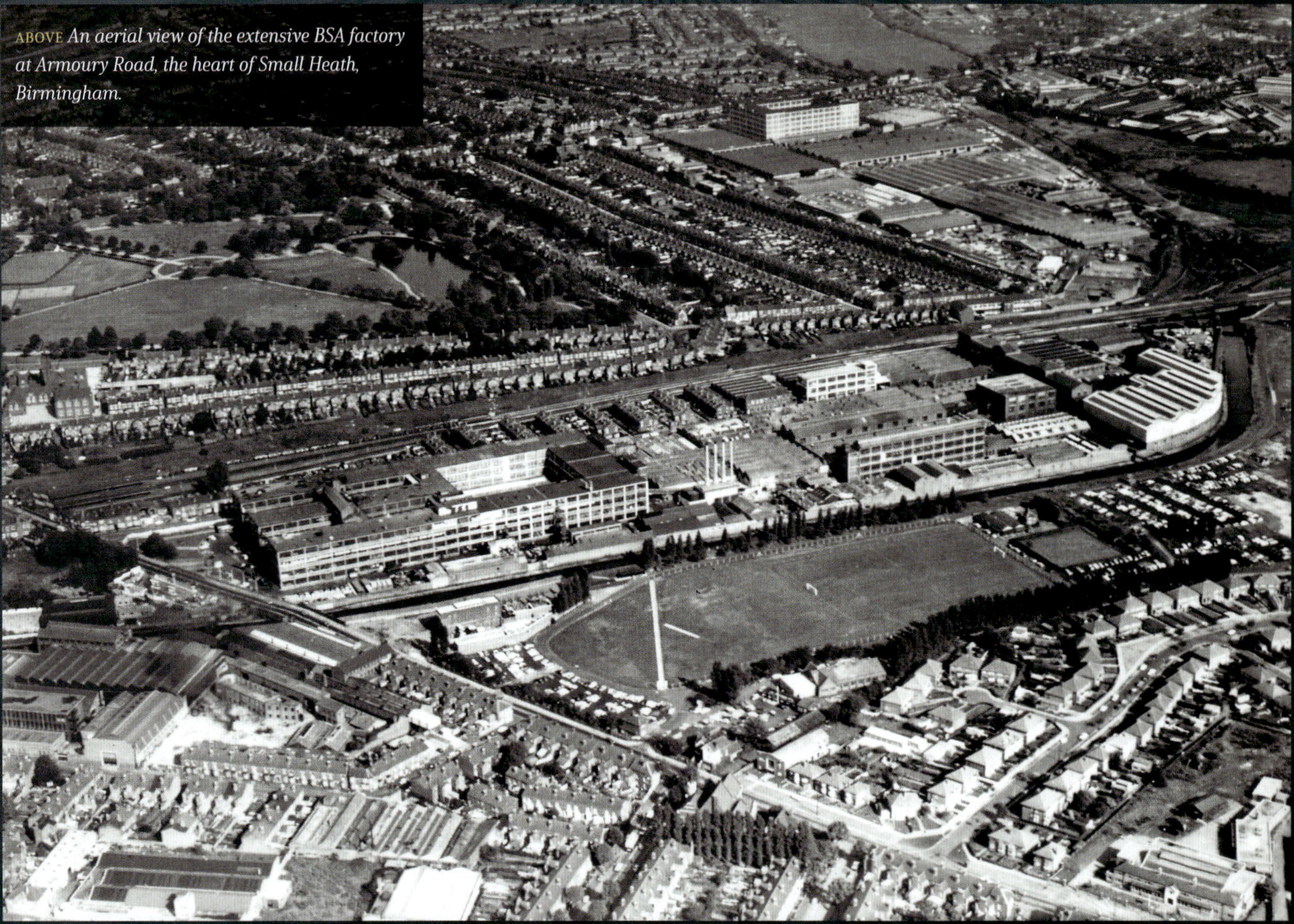

ABOVE *An aerial view of the extensive BSA factory at Armoury Road, the heart of Small Heath, Birmingham.*

During 1970, close to 56,000 British motorcycles were exported to the US, most of them BSA and Triumph. However, under the new, wholly owned arrangements of the group's American subsidiaries, warranty claims for Triumph alone were costing £40,000 a month. Re-jigging US operations had cost £330,000, but new patterns were emerging. Of the £10 million worth of motorcycles exported, only £2.75 million of that was to the USA and Canada. Europe, Scandinavia, and others took an unexpectedly large percentage.

So, machines with unsuitable American-oriented features, skimpy mudguards, high handlebars, small petrol tanks and high compression ratios, were increasingly inappropriate. When a delegation of leading British dealers pointed this out to managing director Lionel Jofeh, he brushed them off, saying he was only interested in export to America. Possibly the group's extensive loans from the banks there influenced his attitude.

THE 'FAR-CYCLE'

July 1970 was lightened by the release of the comical-looking Ariel 3 moped trike, although it was to be no joke for the group. This was an ingenious device, with two fixed rear wheels but a front portion that could be tilted around corners like a motorbike. A British design by George Wallis of G.L.Wallis and Son, BSA had bought the manufacturing rights but not the patent and turned it over to Umberslade Hall. There it was known as 'Trixie', or 'the Pantomime Horse', or even 'the Far-cycle'.

Umberslade brought the two rear wheels closer together, so that it would qualify as a moped in UK law (but overlooked the fact that the trike would only be legal in just three of BSA's export markets). Also, twin torsion bars were fitted, to help the front end up after cornering. Neither modification assisted stability. With a hoped-for production of 2,000 a week, the bought-in Dutch

ABOVE *The 1970 Ariel 3. Even the ads said 'Here it is. Whatever it is.'*

ABOVE *A BSA Fury dohc 350cc twin, one of less than 20 surviving prototypes. Note the use of the 1971 range's brakes and fork.*

50cc Anker two-stroke twist 'n go engine was over-ordered to the tune of 50,000 units, possibly due to error from BSA's computer. Expensively launched, hard to pedal-start and with rumours of instability, the ugly-looking trike bombed, with less than 3,000 sold. This fiasco cost BSA up to £2 million.

BRAVE FACE

Despite that, and industrial unrest at Small Heath for the first time costing 5% of production, plus a two-month strike at Lucas and dock strikes nationally cutting exports, chairman Eric Turner remained bullish. Small Heath production, he announced, was to be doubled to 100,000 units a year. This involved a huge production-oriented reorganisation of the factory itself, with Al Cave persuading all workers to pitch in, since the future of the company depended on it. All areas were re-sited to give a through-flow production system, and an export shipping station was set up at the Waverley Road works for containerised Freightline road and rail links.

The work was completed by October 1970, to make way for production of the new 1971 range. Tooling-up for that had cost £1.5 million, with the factory reorganization itself costing around £240,000. But models from the new range were still subject to uncoordinated development at Umberslade, and production would not begin at Small Heath until December.

Parts were being released from Umberslade without an assembly check or test. A prime example was how the frame drawings of the Triumph 'oil-in-frame' 650cc twins did not appear at Meriden until December 1970. They then proved to fail to marry the engine to the frame satisfactorily i.e. the engine would not fit. This cost three months of pre-selling-season production, with the workers idle but on full pay. The hierarchy had also ignored reports from experienced testers that the new 'oil-in-frame' twins' P10 frame was too high (at 34 ½ in

ABOVE *The sole prototype of a first attempt, by Edward Turner, at a dohc 350cc twin.*

ABOVE *Works manager Al Cave with BSA Group managing director Lionel Jofeh, watching hand-lining of petrol tanks.*

for the Triumph). This was true even for the US, where, as Meriden tester Dave Vaughn observed, "apparently the human race (were) the same size as the midget British."

'EXCEPTIONAL ITEMS'

The group's 1970 pre-tax profit had increased a little to £821,000. But after taxes and what was termed 'exceptional items', the figure was down to a mere £38,000. No one explained the 'exceptional items', which might have been the factory reorganisation, or the fact that despite pulling out of racing and shortly closing the comp shop, £400,000 had still been ring-fenced for the million dollar US race effort. The failure to restrain growth and husband cash flow was leading to a dangerously low level of working capital. Everything depended on a successful 1971 sales effort.

BSA shareholders were not happy. Eric Turner, whom US BSA Inc man Don Brown later described as "an honourable man," may well not have had the true situation communicated to him by his managing director Jofeh, who regularly failed to pass reports on. As author Brad Jones has revealed, when Jofeh had been appointed the group finance director Laurie Beeson, had been 'dissuaded' from involving himself in certain aspects of the Motorcycle Division's accounts.

FURY

One project which Eric Turner had initiated was the new dohc 350cc twin, to take on the very successful Honda CB350, which by 1971 was the world's best-selling motorcycle. Triumph's retired Edward Turner's initial design for the new 350 was fast but flimsy, with a weak crankshaft. But

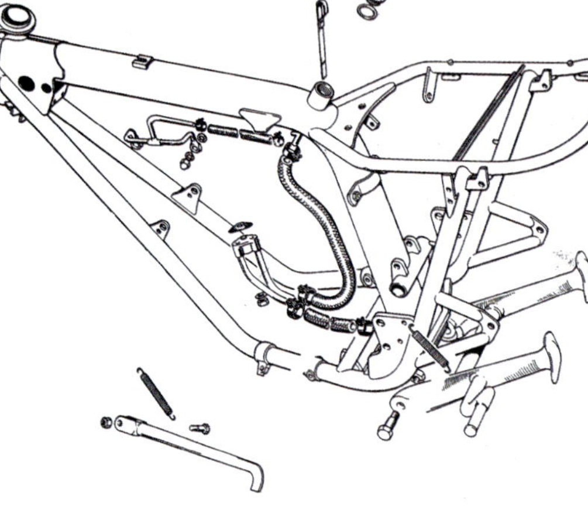

ABOVE *Tall Trouble 1. The early oil-bearing Triumph frame for 1971.*

Bert Hopwood and Hele had done a quick but effective redesign, and in an excellent frame based on the previous Triumph twin racers chassis, the 34bhp twin was now at prototype stage. Component and tooling costs, with 26,000 pistons and con rods pre-ordered, came to £2 million. However, the price was going to be uncompetitive in the US, and Umberslade testers knew that the engine lacked bottom end and was not yet fully reliable. But the die was cast.

Though production was stalled until the end of the year, the publicity juggernaut rolled on, and there was the equivalent of Nero's concert party while Rome went up in smoke. In November 1970, a two-day, £15,000 event at London's Royal Lancaster and Hilton hotels unveiled the new 1971 'Power Set', with the Young Generation dancers and comedian Dave Allen in unusually foul-mouthed form.

The range certainly looked new, with pale-painted frames for the BSAs (Triumph wouldn't go there), a poor imitation of their previous titanium-framed scrambler and of the Rickman's' nickel-plated chassis. Like the latter, the frame carried the lubricant, but with the BSA/Triumph bikes the

amount of oil was reduced to a marginal four pints. There were naked Ceriani-style forks and new conical (but less efficient) hubs and TLS drum brakes. The only truly new models were the 350cc BSA Fury/ Triumph Bandit twins (it should surely have been the other way around? Ed), and in truth they were just pre-production prototypes. The US press and public would be OK with the pale frames, but by May 1971, US dealers had insisted on a change back to black.

By then everything had gone to hell. The 1971 range launch was an unmitigated disaster, limping onto the US market late for the selling season, and bizarre to British eyes. Up to 10,000 unsold machines stockpiled in US warehouses. Jofeh may have been outwardly confident, but there was a Gotterdammerung side to him. In March 1971, when it was clear that the dohc 350 would not be produced that year, he ordered its tooling smashed up, at a cost of £1 million. (Doug Hele: "He did things like that.") He did the same with the well-loved Bantam, despite there being a credible offer to take over production elsewhere. By May, losses of over £8 million were announced for the 1970/71 financial year. Shareholders were warned that the group was on the brink of collapse.

BSA NO MORE

In June, Jofeh was sent to America to sack the extravagant BSA Inc boss Peter Thornton. In his absence, finance director Laurie Beeson finally delved into the Motorcycle Division's finances and discovered a £750,000 plus shortfall in Jofeh's previously forecast profit for April. Jofeh was given the opportunity to resign, which he took, with a £35,000 golden handshake. Worth roughly £350,000 today.

After Thornton had gone in America, the former TriCor boss Dennis McCormack, semi-retired since 1968, took over as a caretaker chief. It seems that McCormack had become embittered, and with the existing long rivalry between the two marques, had developed a deep dislike of BSA. He had the ear of the bankers and of the investigating consultants, and set about advising that BSA should end as a motorcycle manufacturer.

In November 1971, Eric Turner resigned as chairman of BSA Group. In the final quarter of that year 6,286 machines were built at BSA, but with McCormack's advice and the £8 million loss, only 202 were made in the first quarter of 1972. It had been announced in October 1971 that

ABOVE *One of the final, oil-in-frame BSA A65L Lightnings in café racer trim.*

ABOVE *A 1971 Rocket 3 Mk 2. The sun was setting for BSA as well.*

production would move to Meriden and the bikes be badged Triumph (this only happened with the B50/TR5MX 500cc singles). The Rocket 3 was terminated in January 1972, and the last A65 made in December 1972. The marque was dead.

END GAME

The company retrenched from November 1971 with the distinguished Lord Shawcross, already a board member, as chairman. A £10 million bank loan from Barclays, and another £5 million to cover 1972's production, was secured. Sell-offs, of the Alfred Herbert holdings, of the Redditch factory and of Umberslade Hall, which closed in January 1972, were completed. The admittedly overmanned Small Heath

workforce of 4,500 was reduced to less than 1,500. The unions had talked of a work-in, but Al Cave convinced them that the remaining jobs depended on an orderly downsizing. Small Heath survived on contract work and producing components for the Triumph range, especially triples. In the end, the sports ground and most of the factory would be sold to Birmingham council in 1976 and demolished in 1977.

Shawcross was a caretaker, with Brian Eustace running things day-to-day. He persuaded Bert Hopwood to return, join the board and work on future planning. But 1971's £2.75 million loss was just the beginning, there was £5 million more to come due to the downsizing. Interest alone on the bank loans was £20,000 a week. In

June 1972 Shawcross, despite having paid off half the existing debts, approached the Ted Heath government for a £5 million loan to help the group launch a new range.

In November 1972 he was told that up to £20 million was available for the industry, but only if the group merged with Dennis Poore's smaller but apparently successful Norton-Villiers. A 50/50 arrangement was ready to be signed in March 1973. Then a "bear raid" on BSA shares provoked panic selling of them and their value crashed. This meant revised and highly unfavourable terms for the group's agreement with Poore. When the dust settled, the BSA name had gone, and the Norton-Villers-Triumph endgame began.

Tall Trouble 2. A 1971 oil-in-frame T120R Bonneville. The shape of the seat did not help the height.

Norton Villiers Triumph
TAKEOVER

WITH THE NVT TAKEOVER OF BSA AND BEFORE THE BIRTH OF THE MERIDEN CO-OP, ROGER POORE CONTROLLED THE BRITISH MOTORBIKE INDUSTRY.

After the merger and takeover of the BSA Group by NVT, Roger Dennistoun Poore, aged just 57, now controlled the entire UK motorcycle industry.

Cambridge-educated pre-war with a degree in mechanical engineering, Poore had served in the RAF during World War Two rising to the rank of wing commander. He had made his personal fortune as a city financier in the 1950s, where he was regarded as a skilful negotiator in company mergers.

He was an enthusiastic amateur race car driver, RAC hill climb champion in 1950, and in the 1950s drove for Lagonda/Aston Martin. A definite petrolhead, he could also ride motorcycles. He was chairman of Manganese Bronze Holdings (MBH), which principally made ships' propellers. He was a decisive character and, naturally, a right-wing Tory.

Poore himself, approached by the government about merging with BSA/Triumph, not unnaturally had his doubts. But until 1972, previous government funds provided under the Industries Act had been given under Section 7, to maintain employment in a development area. Now money was only available under Section 8, to promote an industry in the national interest. So, if Poore refused the merger, the government might have spent the money exclusively on BSA/Triumph. Poore also reflected that if BSA/Triumph went under, the supply of components from Girling, Lucas and other specialist part manufacturers to his own, smaller Norton-Villiers, might have been curtailed. His new conglomerate would be known as Norton Villiers Triumph (NVT).

ASSET STRIPPING

There were also benefits to the takeover. Under the terms of the deal revised after BSA's share price crashed, MBH acquired

ABOVE *Dennis Poore (Left) with Small Heath MP Dennis Howell on a BSA-built T160.*

ABOVE *An early 1970s advertisement for the 850cc Commando.*

all the group's non-motorcycle assets for £3.5 million. These included BSA Guns, Metal Components, and Carbodies, the company which made London black cabs, and which had recently been valued at over £5 million. The £3.5 million was felt to be derisory, but Poore was a ruthless negotiator and the group had no choice but to accept. Clever setting up of different company structures ensured that MBH would not be vulnerable should the motorcycle side run into trouble.

Poore had been perceived by the government as a successful motorcycle manufacturer, but Norton-Villiers' books had not been scrutinised. The truth by 1973 was different. After a successful 1971 season, for 1972 Norton had launched a new big-tank model, the Commando Interstate. To justify a £60 price hike, attributed to the introduction of a front disc brake, the Interstate along with the range of Commandos, was offered with a more powerful, 65bhp, 10:1 compression ratio Combat engine. With a hot camshaft, the Combat was under-tested and poorly executed – the compression was raised by simply skimming the cylinder head, but the pushrods were not shortened accordingly, and the head gaskets were a liability.

The 1972 Interstate with the Combat engine proved a disaster, with the more powerful power plant destroying the main bearings in under 4,000 miles. The answer was a return to a lower state of tune, plus the fitting of 'Superblend' main bearings. But this involved at least 2,000 Commandos going down the Andover production track for a second time. The Combat ended up costing Norton £1 million.

None of this had made for a healthy balance sheet, and the arrival of the 1000cc Kawasaki Z1 that year had underlined the Commando's ageing nature. In April 1973, Poore simply announced that the Andover assembly plant was to be closed, and total production of the Commando moved to Wolverhampton. In the year of a miner's strike and 'Days of Action', this abruptness demonstrated a failure to interpret the political climate wisely. After a well-publicised ten-day factory occupation, the Andover unions negotiated very substantial redundancy payments. It was a dry run for what was to follow.

Poore did have forward plans. He had brusquely rejected Bert Hopwood's

ABOVE *Pickets at the Meriden gates during the lock-in.*

RIGHT *In early 1975 Triumph T140 production starting again. These are final 750s to be built with a right-foot gearchange.*

projected modular range as yesterday's men. His fairly successful John Player Norton production racing team had led to negotiations with Cosworth to produce an engine, the Challenge, basically two cylinders of Cosworth's Formula 1 car engine. But it proved too heavy and basically unsuitable either for racing or the road.

Hooper and Favill's stepped-piston Wulf 500cc twin was brought to prototype stage, but then stalled due to lack of government research money. This was partly due to the government, since the Feb 1974 election, being a minority Labour one, and money for the Wulf was by then being used as a bargaining chip in the negotiations over the workers' occupation of Meriden.

In the end Poore went

with another asset inherited from the BSA Group, the rotary Wankel-engine machines eventually produced as the Norton Classic and Commander. These were developed for Poore by David Garside, after Norton's main companies had gone under, in a smaller works at Shenstone. Progress was slow due to lack of funds, and despite some racing success, only a few hundred machines would be produced in the late 1980s and early 1990s.

factories. That was why it was the far more successful Triumph factory at Meriden which was selected for disposal, as NVT had had 32 enquiries concerning purchasing it. The plan would also depend on the full cooperation of the workforce.

The offer Poore favoured was that from Jaguar, who he believed would take on three-quarters of the Meriden workforce. He planned to transfer Triumph production to Small Heath even though

THE PLAN

Following the 1973 takeover, Poore had formulated a scheme for the remaining industry. The Grand Plan, as it was known internally, pivoted on the policy then in place of restricting industrial development certificates in the Midlands, which had led to a scarcity of available

previous efforts to do that had not gone well. He also privately intended to make the Commando there, as Wolverhampton had a full order book for industrial engines, but insufficient capacity to produce them. Meriden's labour militancy and high wages may also have featured in his decision.

BELOW *Meriden defiant during 1974 lock-in.*

THE CO-OP

Unfortunately for Poore, the story had been leaked to the *Coventry Evening Telegraph*, and the midday edition was on sale at the gates on September 14, 1973 as Meriden workers and the local Labour MP arrived for an address by Poore. He confirmed the February 1 closure, emphasised that production must continue until then, and as angry reaction began, claimed he had a train to catch and hurriedly departed.

Given the factory and the Coventry area's history of industrial militancy, what followed surely cannot have surprised him. Union officials planned to mobilise resistance and support locally, and the gates were locked, beginning an 18-month occupation. This immobilised around 2,000 motorcycles, often deteriorating in storage, and the situation was soon costing NVT £20,000 a week.

The negotiations went to and fro, with Poore offering to sell the workers the factory, then putting impossible conditions forward, later admitting that he was stalling in the hope that the occupation would collapse. But a core of pickets kept at it. Fear of mass union convergence from nearby factories meant that the government instructed the police, who were on good terms personally with the strikers, not to evict them.

Meriden's fortunes then looked up, for as well as public and media support, Labour won the February 1974 election. Soon the men had radical socialist Tony Benn in their corner as industries minister. More than once he joined pickets around a brazier during the night watch. By July 1974, Benn had negotiated the beginnings of an agreement that would loan Meriden £4.2 million and grant them another £750,000.

Small Heath workers had woken up to the fact that the finite sum of money available for the industry appeared to be going to Triumph and gave Benn a hard time when he visited. Since most of the money went to Poore, as purchase price for the factory and the manufacturing rights, in March 1975 the 600 workers of the Meriden Motorcycle Co-operative started life severely underfunded and would continue that way. Neale Shilton, working for NVT, suggested that any new model the co-op introduced should be named 'The Striker.'

But the only model Meriden could make was the T140 Bonneville/TR7 Tiger 750. The twin had converted to the larger capacity for 1973, which unfortunately had involved de-tuning it compared to the 650 to spare the bottom end, though it was still fun to ride. The experiment in industrial democracy was pursued, with allies including the champagne socialist Geoffrey Robinson, lately head of Jaguar and then a local MP, who contributed his services for nothing.

American enthusiast dealers were supportive. Build and finish quality could be variable, but they improved. Ingenious variants of the 750, either cosmetic, like 1977's Silver Jubilee, or technical like the later eight-valve TSS, were developed and produced. In all around 50,000 more twins had been built by the time the money ran out, in the middle of a move to more economical Coventry premises, early in 1983. There would later be a further 1,200 bikes built by former spares supplier L.F.Harris in Devon, under licence from John Bloor, Triumph's new owner. After that Bloor at his Hinckley factory for some time made completely new modern models, before finally playing the heritage card with the all-new Bonneville twin range from 2000.

 The UK version of the 1977 limited edition Silver Jubilee T140, celebrating the Queen's first 25 years.

 The last bike out of Small Heath was – a Triumph.

T160 TRIDENT

Meanwhile, during the sit-in, Poore had employed several of the Triumph experimental men including Doug Hele, at former BSA premises in Montgomery Street, Birmingham. Among other things, a 900cc T180 Trident, and even a four-cylinder prototype, the Quadrant, were experimented with. But the project that reached production was the 750cc T160 Trident. This featured sleek styling by Jack Wickes and inclined cylinders like the Rocket 3, which permitted an electric start to be fitted. There were also disc brakes all round, and a left foot gearchange to fall in line with US legislation.

The problem was that some of the tooling necessary for production was blockaded at Meriden. By July 1974, NVT losses were £3,670,000. Poore desperately needed product and spent over £400,000 replacing the locked-in tooling. So Small Heath began making motorcycles again, even if they were Triumphs. Launched in March 1975, the smart T160 featured improved ground clearance, but was a little down on top speed due to noise and emission regulations. Some 7,000 were built while the last act for NVT began in summer 1975.

MK III COMMANDO

Norton Commando production had moved to Wolverhampton in 1973. Resentment still existed there at AMC, once Norton's parent company, over the Piatti engine business of a dozen years before. Standards of assembly and finish were not high. The extremely experienced

Bob Manns told how the crankshafts "came in as a casting, the big end journals were machined, and then the whole thing split…Afterwards the halves were put in separate bins – never matched up…"

With the attitude at the top being, quality seconded to quantity production, mainly for export, they even replaced some of the more expensive Reynolds-built frames with ones sourced from Italy. The prototypes had been fine, but the bulk of chassis supplied were varied. Alan Sargent, one of the engineers struggling to improve the Commando, once found a foreman with what was known as 'the donkey's dong', a lead measuring rod for the headstock. When it did not slide through as it should have, the man took a lump hammer to make it do so!

It was Alan Sargent and other dedicated engineers who in February 1975 produced the final 850cc Commando Mk III, most often found in Interstate form. The engine was significantly strengthened internally, oil leaks were down, but the weight was way up at 466lb dry. Part of that was

due to the (only intermittently effective) Prestolite electric start, which along with disc brakes all round and a US-mandated left-foot shift, made it a companion model to the T160, released a month later.

Unfortunately, events very soon cut them both down. In May 1975, Tony Benn was replaced as industries minister by a more centre-left figure, Eric Varley. Before he left Benn had commissioned a report by the Boston Consulting Group (aka 'The Boston Stranglers'). Its negative views on the motorcycle industry's prospects included a spurious figure of 13,000 machines still warehoused in America. Varley in Parliament used this as an excuse to withdraw support from NVT, in the shape of £4 million of export credit guarantees - essentially government money which was paid in advance for exported but not yet sold machines. This devastated NVT and Poore, who had been relying on the promised public funding to pull the industry through.

Shortly afterwards Poore's habit of inter-company juggling caught him out.

 A 1982 T140 TSX factory cruiser. There was life in the old dog yet.

 An early 1990's Hinckley Trident dohc 900, only the name connects it to BSA/Triumph triples..

He had been ordering materials under NVT Manufacturing Ltd (the Small Heath operation) for use at Wolverhampton. A creditor, owed £23,000, tired of waiting and issued an application to wind up NVT Manufacturing. Wolverhampton might have been expendable, but this irrevocable application cut at the heart of NVT's operation and Poore went into receivership.

In August 1975 there were mass redundancies. The 1,700 Wolverhampton workers began a sit-in and proposed to build a new version of the Commando called the 'Norton 76'. But in the confirmed absence of any further government funding, except for Poore to wind down the business in orderly fashion, the Wolverhampton Action Committee conceded, and helped build a final 1,500 Mk III Commandos in 1977, before the factory was sold to Wolverhampton Industrial engines.

In 1975 there was a frenetic sell-off of existing NVT machines at knock-down prices. Most of the final 450 T160 Tridents, in police trim and dubbed the Cardinal, went to Saudi Arabian security forces. It was a Cardinal that was nominally the last machine off the Small Heath line in December 1975, though a few more may have been assembled after that. Then, prior to the factory demolition, the men were let go. For the second and final time, they had seen the heritage, experience and enthusiasm, the best of the BSA tradition, mismanaged into extinction. ◆

LEFT *And then came – the classic bike movement!*

Glossary

A

Ace bars – one-piece dropped handlebars
Alternator – generator of alternating current
AMC – Associated Motor Cycles

B

Bhp – brake horse power
Big end – the end and bearing on a connecting rod which is carried on the crankshaft
Braze – to join two metal parts by heating them and adding hard silver or bronze
Bush – plain bearing, or a lining to a bearing

C

Cam follower – the part located on the operative part of the cam
Camshaft – a cam in the form of an eccentric, rotary shaft with nodes
Capacitor – a large capacity condenser
Coil – an electrical winding in the form of a loop or coil, in practice with hundreds of turns
Condenser – electrical device able to store electricity and release it very quickly
Connecting rod, con rod – the piece which joins the piston to the crankshaft
Contact breaker – an electrical switch, usually mechanically operated
Crankpin – the eccentric journal which carries the con rod
Crankshaft – the shaft which is turned to provide the engine's motive force
Cush drive – the shock absorbing part of the transmission

D

Damper – device which slows down or inhibits the movement of a part
Diaphragm – kind of spring made from a dished steel plate
Distributor – mechanical device used for directing electrical current to the relevant spark plug
DOHC – double overhead cam
Dynamo – a generator of direct current

E

Energy Transfer, ET – ignition system in which power from the alternator windings is discharged through the ignition coils via the contact breaker

F

Flywheel – a weight attached to the crankshaft whose inertia is sufficient to keep the engine turning between power strokes
Four-stroke – an engine cycle made up of four phases, intake, compression, expansion, and exhaust

G

Gasket – a seal, usually soft or compressible, between two mating surfaces

GP – Grand Prix, also an Amal racing carburettor
Gusset – bracket or plate used to strengthen a structure

H

Head steady – a tie-bar between the cylinder head complex and the frame

I

ISDT – International Six Days Trial

M

Magdyno – magneto and dynamo as distinct units but in a common housing
Magneto – a self-contained ignition spark generating system
Main bearing – bearing supporting the major shaft assembly, e.g. the crankshaft
MCN – Motor Cycle News
MIRA – Motor Industries Research Association
Monobloc – carburettor with mixing and float chambers formed in one

N

Nacelle – Triumph's shapely headlamp and instrument mounting binnacle
NVT – Norton Villiers Triumph

O

OHC – overhead cam
OHV – overhead valve. Engine in which the valves are carried inside the cylinder head
o.i.f. – oil in frame, where the chassis carries the lubricant
Oversquare – an engine in which the cylinder bore is greater than the stroke

P

Pawl – a small catch or wedge, which locates in a groove or slot to lock a part
Piston – a moving plunger in a cylinder
Points – moveable electrical contacts
Pre-unit – where engine and gearbox are built separately
Primary chain – the chain driving from engine to gearbox
Pushrod – rod or tube used in compression to move a part

Q

Q.D. – Quickly Detachable, usually where rear wheel can be removed without disturbing rear chain

R

Rear chain – chain transmitting power to rear wheel
Rear-sets – rear-mounted footrests permitting a racing riding position

Regulator – a device which regulates the electrical supply to the battery
Reynolds – principal British manufacturer of steel tubing for frames
Rocker – a pivoted arm used principally to transmit motion in valve gear. Also, a greasy biker
Rotor – the unit carrying the permanent magnets or field coils in an alternator
RPM – revolutions per minute

S

Shim – a piece of strip material used to pack out a part to adjust its position or the load on it
Single – type of engine with one cylinder only
SLS or sls – single leading shoe, drum brake in which the operating cam only bears on the leading edge of one shoe
Small end – the con rod bearing carrying the gudgeon pin and piston
Stator – the plate carrying the power coils on an alternator
Sump – reservoir into which oil can drain. On wet sump engines this doubles as the oil tank
Swinging-arm – double-sided arm moving in an arc to provide rear suspension
s.v. – side-valve, engine in which valves and ports are carried in the cylinder block

T

Tappet – a sliding block or cylinder set between the cam follower and pushrod
TDC – top dead centre
Telescopic fork – two tubes able to slide over one another on bushes with a spring in between
TLS or tls – twin leading shoe, drum brake with both shoes operated at their leading edges
Trailing link – suspension in which the axle is behind the pivot
Two-stroke – engine cycle which gives a power stroke at each revolution

U

Unit construction – a common housing for engine and gearbox

V

Vertical twin – an engine with two parallel cylinders, normally upright in frame

W

Wankel – type of engine with a rotary piston

Z

Zener diode – electrical component invented by Dr Zener allowing a controlled leak to earth above a certain voltage